MW00953794

Island Hopping to the Caribbean

Florida to the Northern Caribbean

By David and Annie LaVigne

Island Hopping to the Caribbean
by David & Annie LaVigne
First edition (version 1.0.4)

Published in the U.S.A. by: David & Annie LaVigne
Book available at: www.captdrdave.com
E-mail the authors at: captdrdave@captdrdave.com
Visit the website: www.captdrdave.com

ISBN 1-4421-0968-8

EAN-13 9781442109681

Copyright © 2009 David & Annie LaVigne

All rights reserved. No part of this book may be reproduced, stored in a retrieval system, or transmitted in any form, or by any means, electronic, mechanical, photocopying, recording, or by any storage and retrieval system, without written permission from the author and publisher. Only limited excerpts may be quoted for review purposes without permission if appropriately credited.

IMPORTANT NOTICE:

Neither the author nor the publisher makes any warranty of any kind, expressed or implied, with regard to the information contained in this book. As with any information concerning navigation and/or cruising, you should consult a variety of sources and obtain as much information as possible. Just as no navigational aid should be replied upon as your sole source of navigation information, this same axiom should apply to the information that you utilize for planning and for making decisions as to where and when you will go. The authors and publisher shall not be liable in any event for incidental or consequential damages or injury in connection with or arising from the use of any of the information contained herein nor can they be responsible for the accuracy of any of the information provided.

All photographs in this book, unless otherwise noted, are by Annie or David LaVigne.

Acknowledgments

We would like to thank the following people for their assistance in the creation and production of this book.

Chris and MaryLiz, from *S/V Wandering Albatross*. If we hadn't been invited to the Classic Regatta we would have missed out on one of our most memorable experiences. Also thanks for the use of that great photo of *Wandering Albatross* kicking butt. And thank you for the use of any other of your photos if, somehow without our realizing they were yours, they might have somehow ended up in this (or any other) book of ours. Oh, and thanks for the *Joker* game and sharing all those great training sessions. And thanks for endowing our favorite sandwich, the *Reubami,* with its name!

Thanks, as always, to Bonnie and Roger, our great and long time friends on the catamaran *Kokomo*.

Thanks to Chuck and Terri. Dominoes , *Rummikub*, or just sundowners in the cockpit. It was always fun.

A hearty thank you to any and all of the friends we met along our way, to those of you who we have mentioned by name and/or boat name; and apologies to those who, as a result of poor records and poorer memories, might have been accidentally omitted.

And to all of the people who have attended my seminars and asked questions and demonstrated that a book of this nature can hopefully serve a useful purpose to those who are giving even some lighthearted thought to making the trip, thank you. Hope you find it useful.

Once again, hopefully we haven't forgotten anyone (like in the first print of *Cheapie-Cheapie*, where we forgot *everyone*) If we have, it was inadvertent (like it was then) and we apologize.

Contents

This book started out as a small book, written as an adjunct to my seminar presentations. For a few years now, in addition to my veterinary seminars that I have been giving at boat shows and other venues, I (David) have been offering a seminar that I always called *Island Hopping to the Caribbean*. The seminar was offered from the point of view of novice cruisers who had never made such a trip before, and was given to describe our adventure as a learning experience, telling, in retrospect, what we felt we did wrong, what we learned from doing it, and just how we would do it next time if we were to actually do it over again.

At first I felt grossly underqualified to give such a presentation. After all, who are we to be giving cruising advice? We're relative greenhorns. We've only sailed for less than fifteen years, the first six years on the Great Lakes where the sailing season is measured in hours, rather than months; the next four years spent living aboard, but mostly dockside, in Baltimore. We've done the trip only one time and are no different than thousands of others who have done it only once. But after receiving the feedback from a few of my seminars, I realized that that is a major part of what makes my seminars so attractive.

For years prior to our departure, Annie and I would go to boat shows, often just to catch the seminars. There we would listen to veteran cruisers, with years and years of cruising experience, talk about things that we could only dream about, trying to relate their years and years of cruising experience and bluewater travels to our little world of dreaming, reading the cruising mags, and occasional weekend or short vacation hops out onto local waters. Try as we might, we just could not put ourselves in their shoes, and their talks often addressed issues that we really could not relate to.

Veteran cruisers so frequently are sailors who grew up on the water. They often cannot remember ever *not* being involved in sailing. How can they have any kind of understanding of someone who grew to be thirty or forty years old, who always enjoyed wandering the docks of a marina *wondering* what it would be like *just to go out sailing on a sailboat?* Do very many of them even have any idea what it's like to *dream* about going? So it becomes a question not only of how the listener can relate to the expert but, even moreso, one of how can the expert relate to the listener?

Very often experts simply know their topic too well. They understand it to the point where they can no longer teach it because they cannot remember ever not knowing what they are teaching. They have gotten to the point where they *feel* their topic more than they understand it. At that point it becomes very difficult to teach what they know, or to relate to those who cannot feel what they feel. It all results in an impression of detachment. And that's what we often would feel when we listened to the *experts* describe things to their novice audience – detachment from their audience.

Well, there is no detachment here. It was only back in 1993 that Annie and I were taking our beginning sailing class from Captain Larry Maples through Delta College, a local community college in Bay City, Michigan. Both of us were in our early thirties and – other than a couple of daysails with Captain Paul on his *CSY44, Island Woman*, down in Tortola – neither of us had ever even been sailing. We had spent enough time walking the docks at every marina we encountered and just reading books and magazines on the subject, and now we were finally on our way. Before the eight week class was over we had bought our first sailboat, a twenty-four foot trailerable. Before the year was over we had bought our second sailboat, a thirty-two foot *Jeanneau*. We were hooked, and there was no looking back.

We were excited about our new life and within a couple of years we were making plans to cruise the Caribbean, plans that involved selling everything we had and just taking off. So yes, we remember what it was like for sailing to be new and we still remember the excitement of dreaming about it and we clearly recall the thrill of getting ready to leave. And we also can remember the anxiety of wondering if we were doing the right thing, of how we were going to do it with so little experience, and of how we needed to learn so much in so little time.

These same concerns nagged at us as we left Bay City to take the Erie Canal from the Great Lakes to the east coast, and as we left Baltimore to tackle the ICW, and again as we left Miami to cross the Gulf Stream at the start of our trip down the thorny path. We clearly remember what it's like to be taking on an adventure that we have never tried. We can relate to what you are getting ready to do and to how you feel right now, and that's what this book is all about.

For some of you hardcore sailors, you might think this book is just a little too basic. But even if you are a crusty old salt, if you've not done the thorny path before, then this book is worth a read. After all, just like every time I go out for a sail I learn a little something, every time I pick up a book and read it, I walk away with some little gem that's worth remembering. You will too.

Fair winds, cheap diesel, & happy sails,
David & Annie

x

To our daughters:
Tara, Jennifer, and Katie
Who were understanding enough to allow us to abandon them
while we sailed off to live our dream

Fidelis anchored off Caja de Muertos – Puerto Rico

Introduction

We can remember the feeling really well. You are all ready to go and you're eager to leave, yet the timing still isn't quite right. Seems like you're just marking time as you wait for the right moment, while at the same time you're taking every opportunity to find out more about what it's really like out there – reading books, going to boat shows, talking with others who've actually done it. Sound familiar?

You've been cruising for a while now but it's been coastal and lake and river cruising. Now you're thinking the Bahamas and maybe, just maybe, if you can find out enough about how to do it, you might try heading on down to the Caribbean – do that trip that you've always dreamed about. Lots of people have done it, and they aren't any different from you. You've got a good boat and you should be able to do it. You just need more information.

What more can you do now to further prepare for offshore travel? How much will it actually cost? Where should you go and how should you get there? Do you really know everything that you need to in order to actually get going? Have you forgotten about anything important?

Hopefully this little book can help to answer some of those questions. It is written from the point of view of novice cruisers. After eight years of living aboard and cruising we were still cruising carefully and we still felt like novices when we were in the presence of seasoned sailors. It didn't seem to make any difference. That's just how we are.

For nearly four years we cruised the waters and anchorages of the northern Caribbean. We did the Great Lakes for a few summers prior to selling everything we owned and heading south, and we spent our first summer of living aboard cruising across the Erie Canal, down the Hudson River and the east coast to Chesapeake Bay. Once we reached the Chesapeake, we lived aboard year-around in the inner harbor of Baltimore for four years while we both worked full time and cruised and explored whatever and whenever we could. And while we were there we continued to fit out the boat for our long term objective of distance cruising. We didn't know for certain where we were going or where we might end up, so we prepared for it all.

We certainly don't claim to be experts on the subject of cruising but, really, is anybody? There may be expert sailors, but are there really expert cruisers? Everybody has their own cruising style. We figure we are experts at doing this the way we did it, as much as anybody else is an expert on doing it their way. We do think we have some useful information and opinions to pass along and we hope we can answer some of your questions about what to expect and what it's like out there.

We are *not* experts on how to get there. But we will tell you where you can find the expert information that you need in order to make the trip. We will tell you how we did it and how we would do it next time if we did it over again. Hopefully, by reading this book, you will be able to avoid our mistakes and by taking some of our advice on how to prepare you can hopefully avoid other problems.

People often want to know what it costs to cruise the Caribbean. When it comes to expense, in a nutshell the answers to all of those 'What's it going to cost?' questions come down to: 1) the kind of lifestyle you choose to lead, 2) how much time you spend in marinas, 3) what you eat and drink, 4) where you eat and drink, and 5) what you do for enjoyment. Assuming you have no major boat-related disasters that swallow your cruising budget whole, we have decided that these are the major factors that influence how much you will spend.

Our cruising lifestyle was pretty conservative. We like to spend a lot of time in remote anchorages, once in a while interspersed with a visit to some kind of hotspot with lots of activity, more as an occasional diversion than as a destination. Partly as a result of this lifestyle, we spent less money than many of our cruising acquaintances, but we did not deliberately cruise 'on a budget.' We didn't cruise cheap; we just have a natural proclivity to live inexpensively. We do it naturally. It's the way we are. So if you pick up a few tips in this book on how to cruise inexpensively, where to shop, and things you can do, then so be it. But our objective in this book is to pass along some ideas on how we made our way south and where we spent our time when we got there.

We left and headed south several years in advance of our original long range cruising plan, so the tradeoff was that we were forced to do it without any income and on a limited amount of money. Did it ruin our cruising? Not on your life. We did limit some of our touring plans ashore and we sometimes searched out the less expensive hotels and restaurants when we did, but that was just another aspect of visiting the places we've been. After all, how bad can it be when you're living in paradise?

Of course, everybody's situation is different and yours may or may not resemble ours. If you have the luxury of a pension or some other more generous income, that's great. We've still got lots of useful information for you too.

So this book really covers two subjects. The first half of the book presents some general Caribbean cruising tips including how to do it at a reasonable cost. The second half deals with how to *get* to the Caribbean *the back way*. If you are curious about island hopping your way down rather than taking the offshore route, or if you are leaving early like we did, before those retirement checks start coming in, then we really need to talk. And there's lots to talk about, so let's get started....

Christmas music – island style.

Waiting for weather, the name of the game...

This seems like a simple question. In reality I think it may be the crux of the entire issue. Once we started cruising in the Caribbean we were continuously amazed at how differently we cruisers view our lifestyles.

When *we* left home we had two principal objectives. Coming from Michigan, our main goal was to escape the winters and the fifteen months a year of cold, miserable weather. We wanted to spend as much time as possible in those warm, Caribbean turquoise waters renowned for their snorkeling and diving and enjoying the beautiful beaches of the region. A secondary objective was to visit and immerse ourselves in the Spanish language and the Latin American culture of the Dominican Republic on the way down. Beyond those intentions we wanted to see some islands and meet some people and hopefully see a little bit of the world. Sailing was a really low priority for us. The actual sailing was a means to an end for us, not the objective of our trip.

We were constantly surprised at how many people zip right past some really beautiful places, don't bother to swim or dive, and seem to be in a hurry to get someplace. The question is, where are they going? As far as we were concerned they were already there, yet they seemed to be on a continual quest for someplace better. For us it took some effort to understand that their interests and reasons for cruising were just not the same as ours.

Some people go cruising for the continuous series of cocktail hours and sundowners and the parties that ensue – a natural carryover of the cruising lifestyle that exists for the weekend or vacation cruiser at home. Many enjoy the tours as they travel ashore on the islands and in the countries they are visiting in order to see the sites and meet the people. Some are obsessed with scuba diving and do little else. And some are there just for the sailing and/or the challenge and adventure of long passages.

Your reasons for going cruising will likely dictate where you go, how long you stay, and your seasonal habits. For us, the beaches, the reefs, and the remoteness of Barbuda were paradise. For some of our friends who thrive on parties and bars and shopping and an active social life, Barbuda was dull and boring and was no more than a quick stopover on the way to the excitement and hustle and bustle of nearby Antigua. And many cruisers bypass Barbuda entirely.

After racing through the Bahamas on our way south (less by choice than by accident) we became slow cruisers. We spent an entire year just knocking around the cruising grounds on the south coast of Puerto Rico and bouncing back and forth from there to the Virgin Islands – Spanish, U.S., and British – and we could easily have spent a couple more years there, but we knew there was much more to see. After nearly four years of cruising we got only as far south as Antigua, and even then we missed some significant islands.

But then, as far as we were concerned we had already met our primary objectives. From there onward, everything else we did was just gravy. We spent a substantial amount of time visiting and experiencing the Dominican Republic and after that we spent uncountable days swimming and snorkeling in beautiful turquoise Caribbean waters and exploring some spectacular beaches. No doubt there were more and better beaches, waters, and reefs further along, but a beach or reef in hand to us was worth a hundred that were further away. So we traveled slowly. The downside for us was that we didn't get as far as we might have. But our plans were to cruise for an indefinite period of time, and eight years of living aboard turned out to be enough for us.

We expected to not particularly enjoy the U.S. and British Virgins. After all, they are over-developed, over-cruised, and the reefs are highly overrated, right? Depends upon your point of view. We were amazed at how enjoyable we found them. Others whizzed right past, commenting on how much better things were going to be further south. Check things out along the way and decide for yourself. You won't know what you might be missing.

So do it your way. Take it a day at a time and have an idea

before you ever go as to why you are actually going. Have fun and, above all, keep those cruising plans rigidly etched in Jello.

Living on island time – Culebra

After the ballgame - Luperón, DR

There are many excellent books available on this subject. I (David) felt that Liza Copeland's books on cruising were very entertaining and highly readable and gave some insight on what you might expect, although they are geared more toward world cruising than they are toward the Caribbean. Beth Leonard has an excellent and very readable book on cruising that deals with many of the technicalities of cruising. Prior to our departure, we read every narrative we could find. Everything you read will contain some tidbit that you'll want to tuck away for future reference.

We have a few recommendations of our own. The single most important factor for our being able to leave when we wanted and that allowed us to cruise affordably was owning our boat. Sure we dreamed of that *Valiant* and that new *Pacific Seacraft* forty and you may too. You may dream of owning that brand spanking new fifty foot cruiser that you saw at the boat show, but the reality is that the monthly mortgage payment may delay your departure by ten years or more.

Imagine all of the excursions, meals out, and trips home to see the family that you would be able to undertake with the money from just the monthly mortgage payment, let alone the insurance premiums. Or maybe you might decide to keep your health insurance and use that money to pay the premiums. Or, if you just put the money away, think about how much longer you could afford to cruise.

There are a zillion older boats that you can buy. Just about any well-built boat can do the Caribbean, but we saw a disproportionate number of old *Morgan* Out Islanders, *Tayana* 37's, and old *Gulfstars* and *Irwins*, and a substantial number of old *CSY* 44's. You can pick up most of these boats for well under $100,000 if you look around and many of them will come fully equipped. Remember, it's a buyer's market and you probably don't need to offer anywhere close to the offered selling price. Catamarans are extremely popular, but require a substantially greater investment than do monohulls.

Beyond the mortgage issue, the pros and cons for getting a

used versus a new boat are numerous on each side of the issue. You get more boat for the money in a used boat, but you also incur many expenses for upgrades, repairs, and refurbishments, not to mention hidden or unknown problems. Often a used boat comes with many of the accouterments needed for cruising. On the other hand, a new boat comes with all new equipment when you choose to go that route, but the problem is that the equipment that comes on it is only a fraction of what you will really need and often is not appropriate for your particular cruising needs. So you usually still end up having to spend a small fortune just adding equipment needed for offshore cruising. And then there is the additional matter of insurance needed on that new boat.

When you do get your boat, check out all the systems, or have them checked out for you by someone who is competent. In addition, get the opinion of someone who has actually 'been out there'. I have attended seminars by 'experts' who really did not have a clue what cruising was all about. (At a boat show one time where I was giving a seminar, I happened to catch a portion of the seminar prior to mine where the presenter, a supposed expert on boat electrical systems, authoritatively warned the attendees that they should not even consider going cruising in anything less than a forty foot boat.) Check rigging, through-hulls, engine, and electrics and make repairs and upgrades wherever needed.

Many experts do not recommend that you do upgrades and repairs yourself, but my (David) experience suggests otherwise. I found that there was much to be gained by doing things myself. 1) We learned from every project. 2) We picked up special tools for each project that would be useful on future projects. 3) We remembered or we wrote down from each and every project how it was done so that I would be able at some future time to evaluate what might be wrong and know where to look for a problem when that system again needed attention. 4) And most importantly, we had the peace of mind of knowing that the job was done right and not done by somebody who (hopefully unintentionally) *thought* he knew what he was doing but was not particularly worried about it since he'd never have to see us again! (Witness the young 'diesel mechanic' in Portsmouth, Virginia at the very well-known repair facility where we had our new diesel engine installed. We found out several days and several thousand dollars too late that he hadn't a clue on how to properly align a newly installed engine or of how to acquire and install a new prop shaft and coupling! I didn't have that knowledge myself at the time and it was just the luck of the draw that I got an 'expert' who didn't either.)

The single most useful book we can cite for taking along on this trip is Bruce Van Sant's book, *The Gentleman's Guide to Passages South*. There is more useful information on island sailing and sailing upwind in this little book than in any other book out there. The mechanics, the physics, the meteorology, and the techniques you need to follow are all in this one volume. This is not counting its other functions which include, among other things, serving as a cruising guide to the Dominican Republic, Puerto Rico, and the Spanish Virgin Islands. We'll say a lot more about this book and our recommended charts and references later, under *Assembling the Necessary Aids*.

There are excellent books on the subject of doing things yourself. For general maintenance references, get Nigel Calder's bible of boat repair, the *Boatowner's Electrical and Mechanical Manual* and Don Casey's *This Old Boat* (because even that new boat that you paid the big bucks for, is now just another 'old boat'). Also the Don Casey book, *Sensible Cruising – The Thoreau Approach*, now out of print, is great. But then just about any of his repair and refurbishing books are worth looking at. Also Ferenc Maté's *Shipshape* has some useful boat maintenance information, if you can get past his sarcasm and caustic wit.

Keep your boat as simple as possible and you limit the number of things that can go wrong and the number of repairs that you will need to make. Every system you avoid eliminates one entire field of repairs upon which you must be knowledgeable. However, only you can make the decision as to how much sophistication and what systems you need on board.

In our travels we encountered those who had avoided installing various systems with the expectation that they would simply piggyback on somebody else who had that particular capacity. That may work fine in an occasional situation, but don't let yourself be a pest. We knew one boat who didn't bother to invest in any kind of weather information or service. When planning a passage, they would just call up whoever happened to be nearby on the VHF and ask for a weather report. Many of us liked to exchange and discuss weather info in advance of a passage, but counting on others for all of your weather and making somebody else responsible for your travel decisions is pushing the envelope.

A less serious situation involves refrigeration. If you should choose to travel without, having no refrigeration does not necessarily need to stop you from buying the *occasional* item that might need to be kept cold. After all, you can simply ask friends to keep whatever you buy in their refrigerator until you need it, at which time you just go for a visit.... Just keep those kinds of requests to a minimum and you'll probably do fine. This is a little less critical than providing weather information, nobody's life is potentially at stake. But, there should be an obvious limit to these kinds of requests.

When you paint your bottom, raise your waterline. The summer before we left Baltimore, we spent a month prepping and painting *Fidelis'* topsides as well as doing a good bottom job. When we painted we raised the waterline. Unfortunately raising the waterline adequately for a fully loaded boat sitting in our marina slip in the protected waters of Baltimore's inner harbor was nowhere near enough to allow for the continuous slapping of six inches of chop, not unusual in a typical tradewind anchorage. After just a year of cruising, our beautiful roll & tip *Awlgrip* paintjob that we so lovingly and carefully applied was bubbled and blistered in many places along the waterline. And we should have known better than to use *Awlgrip* for our bootstripe. We knew that *Awlgrip* does not hold up well to continuous immersion but we just didn't think about using something else.

Besides owning an older boat with no mortgage, another cost saver for us was insurance. This is a hot topic among cruisers and carries ramifications far beyond the substantial expense and the seasonal restrictions imposed by the insurance carriers. If you choose to have a boat with a mortgage payment, this won't be an option. For us, we carried insurance on our trip down the ICW, but coverage extended only as far as the Bahamas. The insurance was reasonably cheap and was sufficient for liability purposes here in the U.S.

When we checked out the viability of insuring our boat for extended cruising we found that there was a reluctance on the part of underwriters to insure older boats and that the costs involved were ridiculously high relative to the desired coverage figures. As a result, we elected to carry on without insurance.

We chose to be self-insured. When you are traveling on a boat that is worth well under $100,000 and insurance premiums, even for a high deductible policy, cost thousands of dollars, it doesn't take many years of successful cruising without insurance to recoup the replacement cost of the vessel. Obviously we cannot recommend this, but it is a viable option.

In lieu of insurance coverage, we chose to invest in adequate, good quality ground tackle and sensible cruising practices. Our main anchor was a relatively small 15kg *Bruce* anchor. We also carried a 45 pound *Delta* plow, and a *Fortress* FX-37 on the bow, both kept readily available for regular use. In our cockpit locker we had a dismantled 75 pound *Luke* fisherman type anchor and, for our ultimate storm anchor, a *Fortress* FX-55. On the stern we had a twenty pound *Danforth* style anchor which we used only rarely.

We had two anchor rodes on the bow. One was two hundred feet of 3/8 inch high tensile chain, while the other was 60 feet of 3/8 inch high tensile with 250 feet of 3/4 inch twisted nylon rode, so that under the majority of desirable anchoring situations we would be able to anchor on all chain with either rode.

I always dove the anchor whenever that was possible. In some relatively murky waters I have dived the anchor where I literally had to get my facemask within inches of the anchor to adequately visualize its position or I would need to do it simply by feel. When our situation or the anchorage precluded diving the anchor, we would avoid leaving the boat if the weather was questionable or if the winds were substantial. And we always attempted to allow adequate distance between our boat and our neighbors to avoid any swinging or dragging incidents. Once we were anchored properly, if somebody then anchored in our lap, we would very cordially inform them that we did not carry any insurance and that they were anchoring too close and were doing so at their own risk.

What about other kinds of insurance? We carried life insurance policies on each of us when we left the U.S. We debated a few times about cancelling them but never made a decision, mostly because we were quite superstitious about suddenly cancelling life policies that we had carried for years. Eventually we changed banks and forgot to change the automatic withdrawal order. As a result the decision was made for us when the policies lapsed.

Health insurance was the one insurance that we were reluctant to give up. We are extremely thankful that we have not had any significant health issues so far in our lives. And in spite of the numerous anecdotal reports that we heard about the free or nearly free public health facilities available throughout the islands and in other countries of the world, we held on to our Blue Cross coverage. This was a substantial drain on our resources but we were just not willing to give up that security. We decided that we would rather return to the States and go to work to rebuild the cruising kitty than give up our health coverage. We have known other cruisers who did give it up. It's a personal choice that you must make carefully. In retrospect, perhaps if we had given up our health coverage, we would have cruised longer. I doubt it.

Know when you are ready to leave. When you are ready to

go, go. Keep your eye on the prize. Don't stick around doing one boat project after another until you've lost sight of your goal. It is easy to get wrapped up in getting ready to go, and if you lose your focus, getting ready has a tendency to *become* the objective. We knew at least two other boats that were preparing to head off cruising at the time when we left our marina and, although there was nothing keeping either boat there, five years after we departed neither one had left yet.

Don't get caught in this trap. Set some realistic minimum parameters for leaving. Go a month after you've left your job, or go immediately after you get the wind generator installed, or use some other event. Event-related times are much easier to meet than specific dates. Whatever you decide, set a departure point. You can always finish your boat projects along the way, and once you have left, you may be amazed at how unimportant some of those projects suddenly become.

Our boat is a perfect example of this change in attitude. We took off when we finished painting the boat. It was our feeling at the time, while still wrapped up in that 'getting ready to go' mentality, that our paint job would not be entirely complete until we had refinished the deck. But we also were extremely eager to actually get going, so we compromised. We took along all of the paint and non-skid for doing our deck, and we had every intention of painting the deck once we got out and underway. Five years later, we were done cruising, but the deck never even got started.

Just leave. We can't say it any more clearly than that!

Motor Yacht *Blue Guitar*, rumored to be Eric Clapton's private yacht.

This is one of the most difficult questions to answer. When we left to go cruising, we left simply to go cruising. We had no plans for keeping any kind of running tally of expenditures. Not only that, but well into the trip we were more or less forced into transferring our finances from our old financial institution to a new one which further confuses any efforts at evaluating our spending. All of this has likely resulted in some inaccuracies in the numbers.

What we can tell you is that during a two year interval extending from February of 2005 through February 2007 our total finances depleted by about $34,000. Obviously that amounts to about $17,000 per year. If you want, you can adjust that $34,000 amount by the Dow Jones index change during that same period to get a more accurate figure.

During this time period and included in the above expenditures were the following expenses: about $400/month for health insurance; a professionally done haulout and bottom job (about $1200); a used *Yamaha* outboard at $800 plus some parts and repairs; a watermaker membrane (about $300) and shipping of a new watermaker unit (about $100); two roundtrip airfares back to the States for Annie, one from Nassau and one from Puerto Plata in the DR; several bus trips to Santo Domingo in the DR and stays at a local Boca Chica hotel as a getaway for us late in the DR hurricane season; $500 or more for roundtrip airfare for two back to the U.S. from Puerto Rico including rental car and fuel; a few hundred dollars spent on Christmas, birthday, and other gifts for our kids and grandkids during that time; several hundred dollars spent on book publishing and shipping of review copies of my (David) first book.

You should note that, other than the bottom job, we performed virtually no significant boat-related work during this time. This was more than offset by the fact that, in 2004 while on our way down the ICW, we replaced our engine and the propeller shaft and coupling, and had transmission and V-drive repairs amounting to well over $20,000. Also, in 1999 while delivering the boat from Lake Huron to the east coast we, as a matter of routine, replaced all of the wire in the rigging amounting to over $2,000. These earlier expenses may be indirectly reflected in the above figures by the absence of any major engine/drivetrain or rigging related expenses.

As was the case with our entire cruise, we had no income during this two year time period. You can get an idea from the above information that, under the fairly average circumstances represented, our annual spending of about $17,000 a year was pretty reasonable and, had we chosen to aggressively conserve, could even have been significantly less. And keep in mind that there are ultra-conservative cruisers out there who are, for any variety of reasons, cruising for probably half that amount. To a great extent, it depends upon your priorities. We felt that living aboard and cruising was, without any doubt, considerably *cheaper* than the cost of living ashore with all of its associated expenses and attractions.

Fresh vegetable truck – Luperón, DR

What equipment is necessary and what you should take along by choice is a topic of neverending debate among cruisers and would-be cruisers, not to mention having been the subject of numerous books. We certainly cannot pretend to advise you on what you need, but we will mention here what we feel is important and works well for us. Some of these things you may already have decided on, some you may still be wrestling with, and some you may never have considered. From what we tell you here and from what you read and hear elsewhere, hopefully you will be able to make choices that are practical for your situation.

COCKPIT ENCLOSURE – One of the most important items that we can cite is a proper cockpit enclosure. You should have a proper canopy, bimini, or awning over your cockpit to allow you to avoid as much sun exposure as possible, along with side enclosures made of *Phifertex* or similar screening material. In spite of all the measures you might possibly take to stay out of the sun – clothing, topical sunscreen, awnings, hats, avoiding being in the sun during peak hours – you will still get more exposure than is advisable. You can't buy back your health. Take care of it.

DECK SAFETY EQUIPMENT - Get some jacklines, tethers, and harnesses to help keep you on the boat when you are underway. We wore ours whenever we were making a passage and were more than a mile or two offshore, whenever one person was on deck alone when underway, or whenever we were underway at night. This is in addition to all of the standard safety stuff.

DINGHY DAVITS or SELF-STEERING – We installed a *Monitor* windvane before we left Michigan because we were expecting to do a lot of offshore passagemaking. As it turned out we did not do the offshore work that we expected and we really missed the dinghy davits that we might have had instead. We used the windvane steering occasionally and it was used extensively when we made the almost non-stop trip back from the Caribbean to Florida, but for most cruising we used our cockpit wheel mounted autopilot much more often. Also we hand steered a lot when piloting our way around the islands. The entire time we cruised, probably more than any other piece of equipment we lacked, we most frequently wished that we had dinghy davits. Give it some thought – it's generally an either/or proposition.

Since we did not have dinghy davits, we hoisted our dinghy from the masthead on a supplemental halyard. It was sufficient for the purpose but not nearly as convenient and hassle free as davits.

LIFERAFT - You probably should have a liferaft aboard. This is a tough decision to advise on. We bought a brand new *Winslow* before we left. Since that time we have spoken to many people who made the decision to buy used liferafts. When we decided we were done cruising we sold our newly repacked and recertified *Winslow* on E-Bay for about one-third the cost of a new one. Our buyer got an excellent deal.

Fortunately no one we know has used their liferafts. But that makes it very difficult to say who might have made the best decision. There is no way to ever know what might be best, and hopefully you will never need your liferaft. The only people who ever get to do testimonials on particular liferaft brands are those who have survived a tragedy. You and I will never hear about the rafts from those same manufacturers that didn't live up to the buyer's expectations.

If you get a reasonably new raft and have it professionally packed and serviced, you should hypothetically be okay. A few cruisers elect to have a readily deployable inflatable as a substitute – not the best way to go. Another alternative would be a much less expensive new liferaft. *Winslows* and *Switlicks* are considerably more costly than many other brands, such as *Avon* and *Plastimo*. Your call.

BOSUN'S CHAIR - Have a good bosun's chair aboard and know how to use it. Don't assume that just because you don't like heights that you can't go up your mast. Fear of heights is a weird thing. I have a ridiculous fear of heights that I think stems from some stupid mountain climbing experiences years ago. In spite of my difficulty approaching the window when I'm safely inside a tall building, I have no problem ascending to the top of the mast when seated in a chair and I can work up there freely and actually enjoy it. I have found the chair to be a valuable item in our ship's inventory. However, if you yourself are not comfortable ascending the mast, in most anchorages you should be able to find someone who is willing to do it for you.

WATERMAKER - Do you really need one? Of course not. Is it going to save you lots of money over buying water from suppliers? Not on your life. Our impression is that a watermaker is a major convenience item. The water that you get from your watermaker may be safer than what you get ashore, whether you buy marina water or bottled water, and it eliminates the question marks surrounding where to get your water. The decision of whether to have one should revolve around the convenience of making your own water. It is difficult to put a dollar value on the freedom from gerry-jugging your water or having to take your vessel alongside a dock to get water. This directly affects your willingness to use water freely aboard your boat.

We used our watermaker the entire time we were anchored in Luperón and other boaters were appalled when we told them. "You use your watermaker here?!!! Are you nuts!" The *Spectra* people told us to use our watermaker in the inner harbor of Baltimore. Man, if you can use it there and drink the water, you can use it anywhere (We didn't use it much there because we had shore water, but we did run it a couple days every few months.).

Many cruisers told us they couldn't use their watermakers anywhere but in clean water. I don't think this is true, but check with your manufacturer. According to the *Spectra* techs, the only threat to our watermaker was in and near the openings of large commercial harbors, where ships have a tendency to dump their bilge water. Oil that is in the bilge of a ship becomes emulsified when the ship pumps its bilge and just a little bit of this oily water can kill your membrane if it gets in, so we were always careful to shut down the watermaker in those situations.

Sure, we had to clean our filters a lot more frequently in

Luperón, and they could get pretty smelly, but other than that we didn't have any issues. And we didn't have the problems that other boaters had who drank the 'bottled' water (That's another story). When we finally left Luperón we tossed those filters and got out some new ones.

Although we never intended to carry a watermaker, we have been really glad that we did. We were certain that we could never break even on the purchase, but we were still glad to have it. Keep in mind that, if you elect to have a watermaker you must run it frequently, a few hours every day or two, to keep the membrane from fouling. Therefore you either need to have a relatively small unit, or you need to have the luxury of plenty of power aboard, a generator or lots of supplemental energy production so that you can make and use lots of water.

If you have a generator you can build your own watermaker that will produce upwards of 30 to 40 gallons an hour for a fraction of the cost of a commercial unit. Instructions and components are available on the internet. These units do work but remember they really eat up the energy. We knew several boats who sold their commercial watermakers and built their own much more efficient units.

WATER FILTRATION - We carried 150 gallons of fresh water divided between two built-in fiberglass tanks. To filter out as much debris, odor, and taste as possible, we ran all of our water through a standard cylindrical under sink carbon filter. In addition we installed a *Seagull* brand drinking water filter on a separate drinking water line. The water that we got from that filter tasted as good as any bottled water we could buy – and we drink a lot of water.

HI-FREQUENCY (HF) RADIO - This is another item we never intended to have aboard. A couple years before we left our marina in Baltimore to go cruising, we had some good friends who were already cruising down in the Caribbean. They encountered someone who was installing a brand new single side band (SSB) radio and wanted to sell her old *Icom* unit. The radio had been inspected and came complete with antenna tuner.

At about one quarter the cost of a new unit, we decided that it was just too good a deal to pass up. Once installed, we used the radio for weather reports, for participating in the regional cruising networks, and for communication with cruising friends up and down the eastern seaboard and in the Caribbean.

If you anticipate having a HF radio aboard and cost is not an issue, you may want to consider a new digitally-compatible model which will allow you to send and receive e-mail. If you want to spend the time and effort getting a license, a ham unit is a little cheaper and allows you a larger selection of frequencies for communication.

WEATHER PRODUCTS – There are now umpteen varieties of weather options out there. Some people chose to use the NOAA/NWS radio broadcast on NMN as recommended in the *Gentleman's Guide*. We just did not have the patience to learn to listen to the synthesized voice and sort through the broadcast info.

For our choice we used two different computer programs and downloaded our information from NAVTEX. The program that eventually settled into using is a German program called *JVComm32* and is available online as a shareware download. You download it and use it and, if you like it and it works well for you, you pay for a registered version. Unlike many free downloads, the free trial version is a fully functional program. We liked this program better than our *Coretex Weather Fax 2000* (from a New Zealand company called *Xaxero*) program for which we had paid a hundred dollars.

Check out all of your options. Often the big difference between options is one of just convenience, but some are much better than others if you intend to cruise long distances.

SUNSHOWER – This was one of our favorite and most-used items aboard the boat. It allowed us to shower in the cockpit and still keep the boat dry down below. In addition the sunshower is almost always nice and hot but never requires any of our on-board energy resources to heat the water. We used ours virtually every day and carried a couple of spares.

If you happen to be living aboard where it's cold and a sunshower is not yet practical, here is an idea you may find useful. While we were living aboard in the marina in Baltimore harbor, we used the shower in our head on a daily basis and operated our on-board water heater using 120 volts. Problem with our 4 gallon water heater was that it was in the aft portion of the boat and our shower was in the forepeak. We would waste a full 30 seconds of water waiting for it to get hot enough for a shower.

We solved this problem by inserting a cold water bypass into the hot water line in the head. We placed a tee under the sink in the head in the hot water line. From there we ran a separate line back to the water heater cold water feed line and placed another tee. We put a shut-off valve at each end of this by-pass (the valve at the water heater end was normally just left in the open position). When we were ready to take a shower we would simply reach under the cabinet in the head and open the shut-off valve for 30 seconds (or until the valve got warm) which sent all of the cold water in the line back to our water tanks. Close the valve and you're ready to take your shower. Voila! Instant hot water! (And not a drop wasted.)

HEAD PUMPOVER - Keep in mind that pumpout facilities are almost nonexistent in the islands. Your boat should be equipped with some sort of means for pumping the head overboard and/or for pumping out your holding tank at sea. In addition you should still be able to make your vessel legal when you are in waters that require you to meet no-discharge requirements.

TOOLS - I (David) carried a huge variety of tools. For starters I took most of the hand tools that I already had at home – my ancient *Craftsman* socket set, a variety of adjustable wrenches and *Visegrips* (one of my favorite tools for universal use) and other stuff. I bought cloth tool bags to have aboard so I wouldn't have to deal with the banging around and the rust issues inherent in metal and even, to some extent, in plastic tool boxes. That proved to be a good move. The cloth bags held up well, stowed easily, were quiet to move around and set down on wood floors and fiberglass decks, and seemed to swallow up whatever additional tools I chose to add. Downside of course was the difficulty encountered when having to dig through a mess of tools in a bag to find that specific item I was searching for.

I had read about significant difficulties with rusting tools aboard a liveaboard boat. In eight years of salt water cruising and living aboard, I didn't think my tools developed any more rust than they would have gotten at home. Of course, I used them regularly (often far TOO regularly for my taste) and took good care of them. But I didn't get carried away with oiling and protecting them and all that stuff. If they got exposed to salt water I gave them a good fresh water rinse and allowed them to dry thoroughly before returning them to the tool bag.

I supplemented my mechanic's tools with various boat-related tools such as packing nut wrenches and a long handled packing removal pick along with various specialty tools which made life easier such as long handled breaker bars for adjusting and tightening my alternator nuts and bolts and a large oil filter type *Visegrip* wrench which was handy for grasping large round items for tightening or removal.

One real luxury that I carried on board was a large tap and die kit that I bought at *Sears*. It came in a large flat plastic storage box and, since it was rarely used but took up so little space, stored away in the deepest, least accessible storage location I had. But when I needed to replace a stripped out engine bolt or add a new accessory on the mast or boom, I already had the appropriate thread tap and did not need to go all over creation trying to find one.

For electrical testing I had a variety of items aboard. Most useful was my small pocket sized voltage tester that I got years ago from *Radio Shack*. I had a variety of supplemental items from a 12-v buzzer with leads attached and a 12-v bulb with attached leads to various probes and alligator clips and long lengths of wire with and without switches to allow continuity testing and powering of various 12-v items. In addition I built myself a small 12-v electrical test unit, built in a teak box and mounted on the bulkhead at my nav station, which allowed me to plug in and power up just about any 12-v operated device, regardless of the type of leads on it, for testing and evaluation, in effect turning my nav desk into an electrical test bench. This was really handy.

I found that my battery powered electric drills were invaluable. I had both a *DeWalt* 12-v standard drill and a right angle version which shared the same batteries. A right angle drill is indispensable for those tight nooks and crannies that are so plentiful aboard a boat. And for maintaining our exterior brightwork, we carried a couple of standard 120-v power sanders. We didn't use them often, but they worked great with our power inverter when we needed them. Finally, for a saw I carried a 120-v sabre saw which I rarely used - but it worked just fine on our inverter on those rare occasions when I really needed it.

Bottom line, when it comes to tools, hand tools or power tools, take what you think you'll need and keep them where they will stay dry. I never had any problems with any of the tools I carried and was almost always able to avoid that frustrating feeling of needing to make a repair and not having the appropriate tool for the job.

THE MAGIC BAG – Under the nav desk, where it was readily accessible I (David) kept a large mesh bag full of items that I needed on a fairly regular basis. I called it my 'magic bag.' It contained some tubes of sealant and glue, rolls of tape including rigging tape, masking tape, electrical tape, the ever present and indispensable duct tape, a medium sized jar of *MarineTex*, and a few jars and tubes of various greases.

In addition we had a shelf nearby which held a bottle of wood glue and some *J-B Weld*, along with a variety of lubricants including, among others, *Marvel Mystery Oil*, *Liquid Wrench*, *BoeShield T-9*, *Sailkote* spray, a spray can and a tub of lithium grease, a can of fogging oil, some cans of butane refill, and of course, duct tape's best friend, *WD-40*. If you have *any* favorites in the world of lubricants, sealants, adhesives, glues, and so forth, make sure you have one with you. It can be frustrating trying to find a substitute when you don't know what you're looking at.

The sailor's emergency repair rule of thumb:

If it moves and shouldn't, use duct tape. If it doesn't move and it should, then use *WD-40*.

For some, this really is the extent of their repair capability. Not a recommended lifestyle. Try not to overdo it.

Kicking back in Jost Van Dyke – Great Harbour, BVI

St. Thomas garbage hounds

The dinghy is your commutermobile. Once you get to wherever it is you want to be, it's your dinghy that gets you to wherever it is that you really want to go.

I have heard and read many opinions on what you really need. There are as many opinions as there are cruisers, and then some. I have heard it said that you need the biggest dinghy that your boat can comfortably carry, and the largest engine that you can handle. For the average, run-of-the-mill forty-foot yacht this may be a pretty good recommendation. Once again however it mostly depends upon what you will be doing.

Our preference and in our opinion the easiest (and the most common) dinghy to own is an inflatable about nine feet long with a rigid bottom. In order to get around quickly and easily, a fifteen horse outboard (preferably a *Tohatsu* or *Yamaha*, which seemed to be the most prevalent and easiest to service where we were) is a great size.

On the other hand many people prefer a hard dinghy with a small outboard. Small outboards are at much less risk for being stolen when you are in those anchorages where theft is an issue and they are much easier to manhandle, while inflatable dinghies are more at risk for penetrating damage when alongside a dinghy dock or when being hoisted aboard. We also saw a few fold-up dinghies and a few people used aluminum rowboats (although, if you have an inflatable, you generally try to avoid tying up next to the aluminum and wooden boats at the dinghy dock).

Dinghies much larger than about twelve feet are often discriminated against at free dinghy docks. In addition, due to the excessive space required, they tend to be viewed with disfavor by the majority of dinghy owners and are thus treated with less care and respect.

Just like anything which is a potential target for theft, dinghies and engines tend to be less attractive to thieves when they look old and beat up, or when they have a very distinctive appearance. Your ingenuity can serve you well in diverting attention away from yours.

If you intend to spend most of your time alongside a dock,

you don't need much of a dinghy and outboard. A rowing dink may be all you want. If you intend to anchor out and take your dinghy on 'road trips' to the local dive sites which may be a few miles away, then you want a nice, stable dinghy with a sizable, reliable outboard.

If you're not sure what you want, then take something reasonably small and cheap and buy what you need once you get down island. Brand new dinghies and outboards can be had for extremely reasonable prices, not to mention duty-free, in Dutch Sint Maarten. We bought a decent used 15HP 2-stroke *Yamaha* outboard from a dealer in San Juan when we were in Puerto Rico.

Bottom line? – there is no bottom line. You decide what you want, or you use what you have. If you decide to use what you have, you will modify your cruising and anchoring routines to accommodate what you have. Once you have cruised for a while, if you buy what you want you will automatically buy what fits your cruising and anchoring habits. Just remember, whether alongside a dock or alongside your vessel, *always* lock up your dinghy and engine and lock your fuel tank and other goodies to the dink. Let somebody else make it easy for the thieves.

With the price of fuel skyrocketing, your fuel tank will become more and more attractive to thieves. When we were cruising I (David) used my sewing machine to make Sunbrella tank covers. In addition to covering all of our on-deck gerry jugs, I also made one for the outboard gas tank and one for the dinghy's spare gas can. As simple as it sounds, even when thieves were stealing gas from other dinghies tied up at the same location, our tanks were never disturbed. Out of sight, out of mind? Or maybe it was just easier to steal from those that were not covered.

Annie and I spent a good deal more cold weather time aboard our boat than we ever intended to. We started our jobs in Baltimore in the spring of 2000 with the intention of staying for just six months and then heading south. It was our first encounter with the impermanence of cruising plans. Hopefully cold weather will not be part of your cruising experience, but if the unexpected should happen, here is what we have to say.

When late summer of that first year rolled around we were enjoying Baltimore so much that we couldn't get ourselves to leave. We decided to stay on. Fortunately it was a mild winter. We were impressed. We faired quite well and the mild winter provided an excellent introduction to the rigors of living aboard in cold weather. We didn't find out until the following year just how unusual that winter had been.

The marina where we lived was one of Baltimore's premier marinas yet, unlike many other marinas where liveaboards are discouraged, *HarborView Marina* had a hundred fifty liveaboard boats, most of whom spent the winter aboard. With the water shut off at the docks for the winter, those boats with people living aboard were moved in nearer the main center pier during the winter so that they were easier to reach with a hose from the main pier. This allowed the marina dockhands to provide free water directly to each boat twice each week during the winter.

We learned to keep the cockpit enclosed and to keep things as snug as possible. We bought shrinkwrap storm windows at *Home Depot* and shrinkwrapped all of the ports and hatches, the vents on the companionway washboards, and the opening into the engine compartment. We installed a bulkhead mounted *Dickenson* diesel fuel heater which cranked out an amazing amount of heat. In addition we used a *DeLonghi* 120-v electric oil radiator to keep the forward half of the boat heated and, when necessary, a small oscillating electric heater to supplement where needed. The *DeLonghi* heater is a great unit since it has no exposed heating elements and no flames.

That first exceptionally mild winter in Baltimore, snow was not an issue and the days were often balmy. We enjoyed ourselves, congratulating ourselves on having traveled far enough south to successfully escape those cold, snowy northern winters. However, the next two years injected a jolt of reality – first a year of record snow followed by a winter of record cold. The water of the marina covered over with a layer of snow and slush and took on the appearance of solid ice. As marina manager, Annie bought and set out bubblers for the marina and strategically placed them out among the liveaboard vessels. We learned how to cope, but the Baltimore honeymoon was over. We kept a collapsible plastic bladed snow shovel on board and also a compact children's plastic toy snow shovel for the nooks and crannies.

Having done so for three years, we could probably write a lot more about living aboard the boat in cold weather and cold water, but we'd really rather not think a whole lot more about it. Hopefully you feel the same way.

When you are away, one of life's principal concerns is, how do we stay in touch with those important communications at home and how do we pay any bills? Even if you have said good-bye to the 'real world' and sailed off with no obligations, how do you receive your annual vessel documentation packet from the Coast Guard and how do you pay for that documentation? If you don't keep your documentation current, suddenly you find yourself unable to get into or out of a given country and your vessel could be subject to seizure.

In order to receive your important documents and communications you need your mail forwarded from a permanent and reliable address. Like many cruisers we chose to use a mail forwarding service. Also, similar to many other cruisers, we sometimes used a reliable and stable family member to receive certain items and send them to us.

We discontinued virtually all publications to reduce the amount of unwanted and junk mail. I even went so far as to drop my membership in the American Veterinary Medical Association (AVMA) because, in spite of my efforts to terminate my subscription to the big, heavy and glossy AVMA journal, the only way I could get it to stop was to drop out of the organization while I was gone.

For certain particularly sensitive items or things that we special-ordered and needed forwarded we would have them delivered to one of our daughters in Michigan and then notify her as to our whereabouts and have her forward it when we planned on an extended stay. Most routine mailings were delivered to our mailbox at *St. Brendan's Isle* (our mail forwarding service) in Green Cove Springs, Florida and we would periodically (usually about once each month) call and have them forward the box contents in its entirety. They, as stipulated in our contract, would pick out any obvious junk mail items prior to forwarding our mail, but nonetheless there were always a few unnecessary items in each mail packet.

Since the Green Cove Springs address was our official address of record, many important items would periodically be delivered there. When we knew it was time for our U.S. Coast Guard documentation packet to show up, we would call them and ask them to look through our mailbox for the readily recognizable envelope (They forward mail for literally hundreds of cruisers.) and let us know if it was there. If it wasn't yet there, we would wait another few days and check again. With other materials about which we were concerned, we would occasionally have them open and examine to decide if it was the item we needed.

Right now we are once again land based, yet we still maintain our Florida mail service because we are still always in such a state of transition. It allows us to go wherever and whenever we want without ever worrying about where the mail is going or who is going to take care of it for us.

Bills and bill paying are another issue. We are big fans of on-line banking. We are also big fans of *Charles Schwab* where you can do it for free. Automatic e-bills are good, and they can make bill paying a breeze. (When you sign up for any kind of automated billing or notification, make sure you check the 'no' box for any and all other 'services' the provider offers in the way of notifications or 'special offers.' These can quickly result in incredible amounts of spam in your e-mail box.)

We kept much of our funds invested at *Schwab* so that we could easily transfer funds from our investments accounts into our checking account whenever we needed to with a simple on-line transfer, and about two or three times a month we would sit down at an internet café and check our credit card accounts. We have kept our money with various investment firms over the years and *Charles Schwab* seems to have them all beat right now with numerous free services, higher interest returns on routine checking and money market accounts, a free debit/ATM card, refunding of your ATM fees, and a whole slew of ways to save money while you save your money.

One thing to keep in mind regarding the use of credit cards while you travel: it may be a good idea to inform your credit card carriers where you are. In today's environment of identity theft and computer fraud, credit card companies get concerned about credit cards that are doing a lot of hopping around from place to place.

Case in point: When we were traveling south through the islands on our way to the Caribbean we used our *TD Waterhouse MasterCard* routinely for most purchases, then once each month paid off the bill through our online checking account, which was at that time through *TD Waterhouse Bank*. When we reached the Turks and Caicos Islands we went on one of our all-day provisioning trips ashore, rented a car for the day, etc. Upon arriving at the checkout of the warehouse food market, we found that, joy of joys, our credit card had been inactivated.

We went and found one of those notorious *Cable & Wireless* phone booths at a nearby grocery store and tried to call *TD Waterhouse*. The phone booth was the old-style aluminum and glass type with the accordion style folding door and a corrugated metal cable on the receiver that forced the caller to stand *inside* the booth. The temperature that day was about 100° F and the phone booth was in the sun.

TDW provided no number on their credit card other than a toll-free 800 number which naturally does not work outside the U.S. It took a while from the Caicos Islands via New York City information but I did get a real number for them. After numerous attempts to get through the corporate phone system's automated operator system, I finally reached a real person and explained my dilemma to her. In her very chirpy voice she kindly responded that my credit card had been inactivated for my own good and my own protection and that all I needed to do was dial this other toll-free number which she kindly provided and all would be taken care of. For some reason she didn't seem to comprehend my situation calling from a world where a quick little tour through the automated answering system of a major corporate bureaucracy was not an easy task, so she put me on hold to transfer my call. At that point my call was dropped and I had to start over.

The second time, which again required the patience of Job

(which had by then drained away into the pool of sweat at my feet) and all of the effort and frustration of the first attempt, resulted in a similar request to put me on hold at which point I lost it completely. It no doubt had something to do with my cerebral temperature rising beyond normal limits but I simply went insane; I started screaming at the woman on the phone as I stood in this 120° F telephone booth in the middle of the Providenciales desert. Eventually, after I lost my voice along with about fifteen pounds of body weight in that island sauna, they were able to reactivate my card and we were able to resume our shopping spree.

This entire fiasco ended up costing us over $100 in *Cable & Wireless* fees on whatever credit card we were forced to use that day to make what should have been an unnecessary but simple phone call, the sum of which *TD Waterhouse* congenially refused to reimburse. I vowed in my response to them that I would pass along this story to anybody who would listen. They have since merged with or been acquired by *E-Trade* to create a new entity that they now call *TD Ameritrade*. When we eventually closed our account as a result of a letter from *E-Trade,* announcing that as part of the acquisition they would *not* be acquiring *TD Waterhouse **Bank*** where we did our banking, *TD Ameritrade* did a fine job of charging us up the wazoo for each and every investment account we had with them when we very prudently transferred all of our funds to *Charles Schwab*. Ah-h, the joys of the indigent sailing lifestyle.

The morals of this long and tawdry tail are several. 1) Let your credit card and your bank know that you are traveling and roughly where you are going and have it on record. That way, when they inevitably screw the whole thing up, you'll at least have a leg to stand on when you ask them to reimburse you for your expenses. I'm certain that Bill Gates and Warren Buffett have to do this whenever they leave town just like you and I do, or they might end up in a phone booth in the desert somewhere screaming just like I did. But they probably have a high-paid flunky to make the call for them. 2) Have a *non*-toll-free telephone number for those important phone calls you might need to make from the bottom of the well. 3) Consider carrying an international phone card.

This was a difficult and traumatic tale to recount and I thank you for bearing with me. I hope this experience didn't turn me into a cynic.

Near Gilligan's Island off Guanica, PR

Looking outward from shore in Christmas Cove on Great St. James Island, USVI

There isn't a whole lot to say about anchoring. We are certainly not experts on anchoring. Frankly we haven't anchored in a really broad variety of locations or bottoms. But we have anchored a lot. In the three years that we have been sailing in the islands we have been alongside only twice and only for a few hours at a time – once in Ponce, Puerto Rico when we were hauled to have our bottom done, and the second time in Jolly Harbour, Antigua where we had the boat hauled and put on the hard for an extended trip Stateside.

I (David) don't know what it takes to make a person an expert on anchoring, but I suspect that once you have dragged at least once in every conceivable anchoring scenario, then you are probably approaching the status of being somewhere close to qualified. We never had that much trouble and I think we were amazingly successful for as many times as we anchored. It is my opinion that part of our reason for this success was that we tended to stay in one spot for reasonably long periods of time and this allowed our anchor to set reasonably well. Also, since we were uninsured, we had a tendency to be particularly attentive to our anchoring situation.

There are a few significant things that we found to be important. Always dive your anchor when you can. Diving your anchor is the single most useful means of determining how well you are going to hold, and, frankly, in our experience surprisingly few boats actually put forth the effort to do it. We were frequently amazed at how often it *felt* like we had a good bite with our anchor, only to find that it was just barely dug in.

It doesn't take very many experiences before you get an accurate impression of what types of bottoms don't hold well. If the bottom is clumpy with patches of grass, you may hold well for a few hours or days. Eventually, however, your hook will plow out that clod of bottom, trap it in its maw, and drag it along the bottom without any oomph left to dig into the bottom. We dragged on a bottom like that in Little Traverse Bay on Lake Michigan and we did it again in the same type of bottom in Nassau Harbour in the Bahamas after over two weeks there.

If the bottom is really hard or is scoured, most anchors will have a problem grabbing. This is where it would be advantageous to have a heavier anchor.

Just how heavy should it be? I agree entirely with Don Casey's view of anchor size and weight. The manufacturer's recommended anchor size for a given size boat has much more to do with selling you an anchor than it does with what is appropriate for your boat. Anchors are expensive, and they don't want to price you out of the market. We went with a *Delta* just one size bigger than that recommended for our boat – and in my opinion it was too small. In general, anchor selection charts are geared more toward finding the smallest anchor that will hold a given size boat under most commonly encountered bottoms and conditions than they are at finding the ideal size. If much larger sizes were recommended, they would be cost-prohibitive for the average boater. Liveaboard cruisers however, are *not* average boaters. We really should carry the heaviest anchor that we can reasonably carry on our bow roller. Why? Because a heavier anchor holds better than a lighter one. It will penetrate a harder bottom, it will dig in deeper, and it will resist the pull of your vessel more efficiently than a lighter weight one. If you have a way to manage it (*i.e.* an adequately sized anchor windlass), get an anchor that is a good two or three sizes heavier than the one recommended in the charts. You're a liveaboard cruiser. Your boat is your life!

Often you can dive and dig your anchor solidly into the bottom by hand when the bottom is soft and sandy. Then just back down a little further. This is particularly easy to do with the light weight of a *Fortress*-type aluminum anchor. Most times you will simply dive and have a look at your anchor and signal your mate to just back down a little harder, if anything at all. But it is amazing how often you think you've backed it down well and that you have a good bite, and when you visually inspect it, you find it's not that good at all.

Sometimes the water is just too murky or too nasty to dive. In this case we use what we feel is the best anchor choice, back it down solidly, and then stay aboard for at least an overnight before we are comfortable leaving the boat.

In mangrove waters where it's too murky to see well, be careful if you dive your anchor. Wear gloves. In this type of water you will often find a critter that lives on the bottom that looks like an upside-down jelly fish – and that's exactly what it's called. It may be an anemone of some sort. Whatever it is, it will inflict some serious stings if you inadvertently place your ungloved hands into it. Just disturbing it while hovering in the water above it can cause it to release stinging cells that may result in some serious discomfort to your unprotected face.

In mangrove mud, such as Luperón in the Dominican Republic or Salinas, Puerto Rico, a *Bruce* type anchor is generally your best bet. In Luperón, plows often seemed to drag when the wind piped up. A *Bruce* or *Danforth* type didn't. We saw one large 60 foot boat that couldn't hold with their large *CQR*, but a 60 pound *Bruce* did the trick. And we sat in the yacht club one day watching a delivery skipper with a 37 foot *Hunter* try five times in a row to get his plow to set with the trades blowing stink. If the trades are blowing hard, a *Danforth* type is your quickest solution.

Always try to dive your anchor whenever possible.

In Fat Hogs Bay on Tortola and in the water of the Cayos Caribes near Salinas on the south coast of Puerto Rico, the water was turquoise but extremely murky. It required several dives and a hand-over-hand trip along the anchor chain to even *find* the anchor. Then, because visibility was near zero, it was necessary to *feel* the anchor to see if it was properly set.

More recently, once we were in the real tradewind latitudes, I became a big fan of my *Fortress* anchors. The *Danforth* type anchor, when properly set, has the greatest holding power of all the common anchors. And when you are in a situation where the wind is not likely to shift more than a few degrees at a time, there is really no force likely to break it loose. When you combine this with the light weight and large size of an aluminum *Fortress* anchor it amounts ᵗᵒ a no-brainer. My only issue was coming up with a way to stow it in my bow roller. I could get it through to the point that it stuck up about 30° to the deck. I then tied it off with a couple of lanyards. It looked goofy, but who cares? My back loved it when I would haul it up by hand.

We carried a seventy-five pound collapsible *Luke* fisherman type anchor stowed in pieces in the cockpit locker. When fully assembled I could barely pick it up. We had it for that ultimate emergency where we might find it necessary to hook ourselves to a rock or coral bottom. I had it fully assembled in the dinghy on a couple of occasions but I was always reluctant to drop it in the water since I was afraid that once it went in, I'd never get it back aboard with our manual windlass and my lousy back. But still, it was there if we needed it.

When we were on the Great Lakes I fell in love with our *Delta* anchor. We bought one for our thirty-two foot *Jeanneau* and used it all over Lake Huron and in the North Channel of Ontario. The plow concept seemed very logical but I was scared to death of the hinges on a *CQR*. Doing surgery and playing guitar are my livelihoods. I didn't want to lose my fingers. Our hingeless *Delta* seemed to always do well in the sandy bottoms of Lakes Huron and Michigan where we sailed, but once we got to the Bahamas I began to lose confidence.

After a few incidents of having our *Delta* fail to set, I began to experiment with our relatively undersized *Bruce*. The *Bruce* was the acknowledged anchor of choice in Luperón in the DR, so when we left there we just continued using it. In crowded anchorages I began to dive not only my own anchor but those of other nearby boats. Since the *Delta* is extremely popular in the Caribbean, particularly on charter boats but also among many cruisers, I was able to check a lot of them. I found that about half the time, regardless of how the boats backed down on them, they seemed to lie on their sides and not set properly – the exact issue that I felt we had. I found that most of the time in Caribbean sand bottoms our 33 pound *Bruce* anchor set far more effectively and reliably than our 45 pound *Delta*. Plus, I found it much easier to manhandle that little 33 pounder in fifteen feet of water and dig it into the bottom when necessary, than to do that with the unwieldy 45 pound *Delta*.

But you need to decide for yourself. I don't expect you to take my word for it.

One more thing. We painted all of our anchors with white paint. It is a habit that started many years ago when we bought our *Luke* anchor. Paul Luke suggested it to us as a way to make our anchor easier to see in addition to providing an extra layer of protection over the galvanizing. When cruising the Great Lakes our white anchor was always easy to see in the crystal clear water, regardless of the depth. The same holds true for most Caribbean anchorages.

What about an anchor for your dinghy? There are a plethora of articles on anchoring your yacht and a number of books on the subject, but I don't know if anybody discusses anchoring your dinghy.

We used a relatively lightweight (maybe 5 pounds or so) folding grapnel. Occasionally we considered using something else. Several years before we used to use a plastic-coated mushroom. I don't have any idea why we changed. Maybe because the grapnel folds up; I don't remember.

The important part of anchoring a small lightweight dinghy is to have a chain leader on your dinghy anchor. If you anchor outside of the surfline, the anchor type probably won't make much difference, since it seems to be the weight of the chain that actually does most of the holding. I don't think the anchor makes near as much difference as the chain does.

Most times when we anchored our dinghy, it was because we were snorkeling; so we almost always got to observe how it held. Typical scenario: We would find a spot, stop the engine and try to lower the anchor onto clean sand bottom. I would get in the water and, while snorkeling on the surface, grab the anchor rode in hand, lift the anchor and chain and carefully guide it to a sandy spot where the chain was not going to damage any coral. I would then carefully set the anchor and chain on the sand and we would leave it. While we were off enjoying the sights, the lightweight inflatable would ride the waves with little or no resistance, and when we came back an hour or two later, regardless of wind and waves, the chain would still be in the same pile on the bottom as when we left. Just about any dinghy anchor would work equally well in this situation. Just make certain you carry adequate rode.

Another anchoring scenario involves when you approach the dinghy dock. One person gets out of the bow and steps onto the dock holding the painter and the locking cable. This person, while holding painter and cable, then pushes the dinghy away from the dock while the coxswain in the stern of the dink drops the anchor off the stern. The person on shore then pulls the dinghy back in, stretching the stern rode and chain, to allow the coxswain to step ashore. When you tie off the painter and lock the cable, the dink then settles back on the anchor rode well away from the dock and the other dinghies. This makes your dink and any items in it much less attractive to thieves and gives it a little breathing room away from the rest of the dinghy dock crowd.

If you leave your dinghy on a beach, then the anchor can be an important factor. Ideally, rather than relying on an anchor, you want a long painter that you can tie to a tree or rock. Tree and rock being absent, your second choice is to pull the dinghy far onto the beach and take a heavy grapnel or a *Danforth* or a *Bruce* or plow far up onto the beach and set it deep into the sand. Again, a substantial length of chain will significantly reduce the necessary heft of the anchor. Just keep in mind you have to lug that chain around in the dinghy wherever you go. I think we had maybe ten or fifteen feet of about ½ inch chain – overkill for many situations, but better than chasing our dinghy off into the horizon.

Our preference when taking the dinghy to the beach was to anchor it offshore in a few feet of water with plenty of scope, let it drift back to where we could easily jump out into something less than waist deep water, then walk to shore. This is not always possible if the beach is really steep to, but it results in far less wear and tear than the beating of being dragged up and back down the sand and having the surf beating against it. If we found it necessary to drag the dink onto the beach, we liked to pull it far enough ashore to allow turning it bow-to to the waves so that we could avoid water breaking over the transom. Your dinghy takes such a beating day in and day out that every little bit of relief will help extend its useful life.

Coral Bay, St. John, USVI – in the rain. The hurricane hole tucks way back in to the near left in this photo. Since this hurricane hole is so small (limited to less than a dozen boats or so), and it lies within the boundaries of a national park, access to it is limited. When we were in the USVI, boats had to be signed up in advance and the successful applicants were chosen by lottery.

What can a veterinary doctor and his wife tell you about taking care of your boat? Not much that you probably don't already know, if you've done your homework. Read everything you can on this subject. Get Nigel Calder's huge maintenance book and look it over. Then keep it on board.

Go to those diesel maintenance seminars that they offer at the boat shows and the gams. We have both attended more than one of these seminars, not to mention a professional diesel class for boaters offered at a local community college prior to taking off on our cruising career.

Treat your diesel fuel. With both of us having been to a number of seminars over the years from the Great Lakes to Florida, we understand that the experts don't always agree on everything. However, we can think of three things that they ALL have agreed upon: 1) You should change your oil – *often.* 2) You should treat your fuel to kill any algae growth, and 3) you should keep your diesel tank as full as possible to reduce condensation which leads to algae growth. Under humid conditions, nasty stuff will grow in it if you don't do these two things.

A couple of these guys have mentioned *Biobor* by name, but there are some similar products that have come along since then that may or may not be comparable, so check it out. Be aware that if you use too much *Biobor*, it can ruin your engine. It will eat your seals and any other rubber type plastic parts with which it comes into contact. This is a simple case of what I (David) tell my veterinary readers in my veterinary books: just because a little of something is good, does not mean that a little (or a lot) more will be better. Often it's quite the opposite.

We had a cruiser acquaintance we met while out cruising. We were in a Caribbean harbor together for hurricane season and one day we were talking about fuel and about why we were buying fuel to top off our tank. He thought that buying fuel in that harbor was a bad idea. I explained that we were using our Baja filter to filter the fuel as we poured the diesel fuel into the tank, and I commented that I had found no solid matter and no water, actually nothing objectionable at all, in the fuel. He said that if you get your fuel from a reliable source you don't need to filter it. Since the fuel we had bought there in Luperón actually looked significantly better than a batch that we had bought (and filtered) at a very popular marina in Miami Beach, I bit my tongue on this, wondering, if we wasn't looking, how he knew when a place was 'reliable' when he had never been there before.

As I was treating my fuel with *Biobor*, he warned me that he had read a posting on an internet bulletin board that treating your fuel was not a good idea. He had never attended any type of engine class or seminar but he had read a note posted by some overzealous boatowner who had destroyed his engine by using an algacide. As a result of these 'informed' opinions he was out cruising without filtering or treating his fuel, his vessel sitting in the tropical summer heat in a harbor for several months with a half empty fuel tank. But, who are we to comment; last thing we heard he had made it all the way to Grenada and was still doing okay.

So we all make our own choices and we live with them. As one cruising friend of ours said: "That's why we all have our own boat."

Change your oil frequently. We try to change oil at least every 100 hours. Our engine right now has about 700 hours on it and we have changed the oil probably 10 times since we first fired it up. We have always tried to carry about three or four oil changes' worth of oil and at least that many new filters.

We had a rigging specialist come and check out our rig a couple months before we left Baltimore. One of his recommendations, that we replace all of our lifelines, was high on our list of things to do. He recommended that we replace them with bare wire lines rather than the more cosmetic plastic coated ones, advising us that the plastic coating tends to shorten the life of the stainless steel. Following his advice also made the lines a little less costly.

Check out the electrical system on your vessel. I added a number of new circuits and have replaced some others. I have not been good about removing the old circuits that I have replaced, mostly because I didn't want to take the time and the effort. It can be very time-consuming and tedious trying to track down both ends of a mystery circuit and then trying to remove it without inadvertently disrupting some other line.

I added some megafuses to the main power lines to hopefully prevent the boat from catching on fire in the event of an accident. And I have added a few smaller in-line fuses and a couple of smaller breakers near the battery bank to also aid in this regard.

One significant improvement that I made was the addition of a large, heavy-duty busbar for the positive pole and another large busbar for the negative pole of my battery bank. This makes for much cleaner and safer power distribution with more secure fittings. It also more easily allows the addition of a new circuit if it must feed directly from the battery bank.

How much battery power do you need? This is a major question that really depends on how power hungry your setup is. I recently spoke at a boatshow where I sat in on a seminar given by a marine electrical 'expert.' He stated that you should not go cruising in anything less than a forty foot yacht and that you could not live comfortably with less than 800 amp hours of power. He should tell that to all of the thirty foot boats out there, many of whom are cruising with minimal electrical use. I seriously doubt if he had ever done any cruising; but he was an 'expert.'

We had about 650 amp hours on our boat and, frankly, we had a more power-hungry energy setup than a lot of boats. If we had not had our energy-hungry little 12-volt *Polar Mate* refrigerator, we could probably have sat for weeks in an anchorage without running our little generator, as long as we had some sun and a little breeze. Even with the refrigeration running, we were still okay for days at a time, unless we got a period of cloudy windless days.

Look over Nigel Calder's book and check out what he says. He actually cruises and has been for a thousand years. His book will give you some actual methods for calculating how much energy you may need, depending upon your desired setup. His knowledge comes from somewhere other than out of left field and is not just some kind of speculation on what cruisers should hypothetically be doing.

My suggestion is that you get what you think you will need in the way of electrical storage and production and then cruise for a few weeks or months close to home. If you come up short, you can still either add some additional energy generation capacity or add some more batteries while still able to pick them up conveniently and cheaply. Or you can strip some of the energy gobblers off your boat.

Carry spares. You should carry as many as you can without giving up too much valuable food and supply storage space. We carried three spare high-output alternators and I would have about one alternator rebuilt each year. We carried a variety of engine spares and also carried rigging spares and watermaker spare parts. I had bags of small parts, screws, bolts, nuts, plumbing and electrical supplies, and so forth. In addition we carried a huge selection of tools, both power and manual, a Sailrite sewing machine, and a variety of fabrics. The more stuff you carry, the more likely you'll be able to repair it when it breaks, or at least jury-rig something until you can get the right stuff.

When we were in Puerto Rico, we began to have problems with our refrigerator compressor. I went to the local autoparts store and bought some 134a coolant to recharge the unit and a recharging kit. Since my refrigeration unit was brand new (a little *Polar Mate* – same compressor type as the small *Adler-Barbour* units) when we left the States, I had not really prepared for this problem. In Puerto Rico you cannot buy refrigerant from most autoparts stores without a license, but you can readily buy it at *Wal-Mart, Sam's Club,* and at *K-Mart*. So I bought a case of it to have aboard and we recharged our way across the northern Caribbean until we finally got to Antigua.

In Antigua I began to feel a little guilty about using up ten years' worth of 134a refrigerant in a matter of a few weeks, even if it is more environmentally friendly than freon, so I found a local refrigerator repair guy. I explained my problem to him over the phone and he sounded knowledgeable. Next day when I met him at the local chandlery to pick him up, he seemed to already know what my problem was before he even came out to the boat.

I brought him out in the dinghy, showed him the compressor and he explained that this problem was very common in these compressors. He had already repaired several this cruising season. His explanation? Evidently the solder that they use when assembling these units tends to break down in the salt water environment and eventually all the joints in the tubing leak. A little soap solution on the subject readily demonstrated this (something I had already done but missed). Simple problem. His solution? He disconnected the compressor, took it home with him for the night, and resoldered *all* the solder joints.

He recharged it and it worked like new again. No more leaks, no more repeated recharging. Anybody out there need to buy half a case of 134a?

Approaching squall, Simpson Bay Lagoon, St. Martin

We heard the bad news when we were in Puerto Rico. Some friends of ours who had spent several months anchored next to us in the Dominican Republic had their boat blow onto the rocks in Bahía Samaná on the east end of the DR. The boat was a meticulously maintained, beautiful 49 foot *Vagabond* ketch. We were shocked and saddened when we heard the news and we were eager to hear how things went and whether they would be able to keep cruising.

They had left Luperón a couple weeks or so after we left. As is commonly done by many cruisers, sometimes by choice and other times dictated by the weather, they had stopped in Bahía Samaná, the large V-shaped bay at the east end of the island of Hispaniola.

Several factors came together to lead to their problem. They were at anchor, and on their anchor they had one of those little bullet-shaped shackles that are designed to pass through your bow-roller easier than the traditional bow-type shackle. In addition the shackle was made of stainless steel. Now that shackle design is purported to be not quite as strong as the traditional anchor shackle, and, in addition, stainless steel parts tend to have less strength than do galvanized parts. So they had an inherently weaker link in their chain than they might otherwise have had.

What then ensued might be described as a series of unfortunate events. While at anchor they had been polishing their fuel and, as it turned out, evidently didn't bleed the fuel lines properly when they finished. This led ultimately to engine starting difficulties when a squall suddenly blew in and swung them around in a direction they had not prepared for. When the anchor chain suddenly parted at the shackle and the engine wouldn't start, they ended up in shoal water sitting on the rocky bottom with a measurable hole in the side of the boat below the waterline and with the boat resting somewhat on its side.

At some point after this incident, they contacted a local boat to help them refloat the boat and had what they felt was a tow. However the locals who helped them did not see it that way, and they presented them with a salvage bill for US$10,000 which they had no choice but to pay or lose their boat. Another mistake.

This is one of those stories you hear about and always vow you will never let happen to you, but when you are desperate and don't have any choices and there is a language barrier, sometimes it just doesn't work out as planned. So, grudgingly, they paid. And they and we and you and anybody else who has heard their story have hopefully learned something.

One final comment that is worth remembering. While they were in the process of refloating the boat, a friend of ours (and theirs) dove on the boat to repair the hole. He took with him a *battery-powered* hand drill and he actually managed to drill and screw in a dozen large screws *under water* – enough to successfully patch the hole – before the drill finally burned up. I would never have even considered trying this maneuver, let alone expected it to be successful. Food for thought.

(By the way, do take note that I said BATTERY POWERED and not a standard inverter powered plug-in type drill. I accept no responsibility for anybody's injuries who has misread what I just wrote.)

Happy ending. They did finally make their way across the Mona Passage to Puerto Rico and had some repairs done in Ponce. From there they moved on to the BVI where they ultimately had the vessel completely repaired good as new, and last thing we heard, they were all the way down in Grenada. Maybe they should rename their boat *Perseverance*.

So how do you cruise on the cheap? What do you do and what don't you do? Well, just like us you'll do whatever you want to do, I'm sure. But here are a few ideas of how we did things and ended up spending a lot less than a lot of other people. Again, our entire cruise was not focused on saving money. It just turns out that we tended to live a little different lifestyle when we were cruising than do many others.

We pretty much simply lived life like we do when we're home. We're never very big on doing a lot of commercial things that are advertised. When we travel at home we don't stop in and see the local sights and the local tourist traps; we don't stop and visit every battlefield and historic site that pops up, and we carefully pick where we stay overnight and how much we spend. That's just the way we are.

Contrast that standard of living to how you or your friends live when you are off on vacation or on a charter trip or you are visiting somewhere for a relatively short time on a more or less luxury budget that you have allocated specifically for that given trip. Eating most of your meals in restaurants, often or occasionally relatively high end compared to your standard at-home eateries, buying souvenirs, taking excursions, all with considerably less attention to cost than when you are at home. It's the common 'vacation mentality.' This seems to be the way a significant number of cruisers live.

So a lot of our savings when cruising, we think, tended to revolve around what for us is just our lifestyle. We didn't cruise like we were on vacation or on a charter trip. We didn't eat and drink out any more when we were cruising (actually we did it much less) than we do when at home and, other than the occasional car rental, we almost always used the cheapest form of mass transportation to go wherever it was that we wanted to go. Public transportation did not just save us a substantial amount of money; it was entertaining and informative and allowed us to interact with the locals. Not to mention we almost always ended up with a great story to tell.

When we are home we go out to eat once in a while – for

Mexican food, to a good burger joint, for good Italian, or whatever – but we tend to avoid the more expensive chains and only rarely (and I mean *rarely*) do we ever go out and spend a day's pay to eat out. When it comes to eating out, it's not that we're cheap, it's mostly that we don't like to be disappointed and we don't like to feel that we didn't get our money's worth. Frankly, for us it takes a really special restaurant with outstanding cuisine and a really special ambience to be worth dropping a hundred and fifty bucks, because almost always the food is inferior to what we could prepare ourselves at home. And this truth is even more applicable as you cruise the islands.

It seemed to us that every wannabe chef from Wotsit, Belgium to Stix City, Montana has settled in the Caribbean and opened a high end restaurant in Tortola, in French St. Martin, in the Dominican Republic, or wherever you happen to be. Many cruisers are lining up to eat at these places and the food, in our experience, especially for the prices they charge, seemed to always be not much better than just okay.

There was an interesting little outdoor Mexican restaurant in Dutch Sint Maarten not far from the dinghy dock, near the bridge into Simpson Lagoon on the Dutch side. It was owned by a Latino couple, she was from Colombia and he from Mexico. The Mexican food was novel and good, it was economical, and we got to try her version of the national food of Colombia. Sitting outside at picnic tables on the side of the road though, does not really qualify as fine dining.

On the French side we spent a few days anchored in Baie Grand Case, on the northwest shore of the island, where they have the most French restaurants of any town in French St. Martin. One night each week during the winter tourist season, Grand Case closes down its main street to vehicular traffic and the town takes on a carnival atmosphere with souvenir vendors lining the entire length of the street – definitely a worthwhile stop and good entertainment for an evening. And its entirely free unless you want to buy some souvenirs or eat in one of the local continental style restaurants, where they really do entice you with some excellent values for your American dollar. One helpful thing about being on a small boat is that the temptation to buy souvenirs tends to be tempered by the question of where you will put them.

There in Grand Case they also have a little cluster of barbeque restaurants, on a pier right next to the water, serving excellent food at really good prices. This is where many of the locals eat and the food is an excellent value.

We have a very small but nice galley aboard *Fidelis* with a three burner stove and an oven and we can prepare meals on board that blow most of those restaurants away. And the ambience of eating in the cockpit with a nice trade wind breeze and with the sun reflecting off the water or the sun going down over a mountain range is phenomenal. That's a lot of what we enjoyed about our cruising. It made little difference whether we'd prepared steaks or rack of lamb on the grill, linguini prima vera from fresh ingredients we just bought at the local market, or a fresh grilled chicken Caesar salad – it all tasted even better when we were on board. Combine that with a good bottle of wine and it just doesn't get any better.

And breakfast in the morning in the cockpit is one of cruising's wonders. We ate other meals ashore sometimes as a convenience or when we had a particular craving (like your typical junk food urge) for something that we just couldn't do. But we almost never ate breakfast ashore. Sometimes it was just a bagel with one of the local jellies, sometimes it was bacon or sausage with eggs, and, on occasion, it might be omelets. It was special and it was fun and it became one of those wonderful moments when we could look around at our special circumstances and truly appreciate where we were and the unique nature of what we were doing.

On Thanksgiving and Christmas, Annie always made a turkey – yes, a full-sized real-life Thanksgiving turkey dinner with stuffing, cranberry sauce, green bean casserole, home made scratch mashed potatoes and gravy, and home made apple pie. She did this every year for the eight years that we lived aboard.

Sometimes we would spend the holiday by ourselves, but usually we invited friends over from nearby boats to share in our feast.

In 2005 when we left Luperón, it was only a few days before Thanksgiving. (That was the year of the longest hurricane season in history - when they actually ran out of letters to name them.). When we arrived in Boqueron, Puerto Rico, we ran into another friend from Luperón who had arrived the night before and who had a taxi on its way to make the drive to Mayaguez to check in. We split the cab fare with him and on our way back from checking in we had the cab driver stop at a grocery store so we could get a turkey to make the next day for Thanksgiving dinner. Unfortunately we were too late to get anything but a twenty pounder or bigger. All the smaller ones were gone. So we bought a duck – outrageously expensive, but tradition is tradition, right?

The next day we had a wonderful Thanksgiving celebration in the cockpit, as another three boats from Luperón had shown up the previous day while we were in town and we invited them all over for dinner. We enjoyed ourselves tremendously mostly because we were all feeling festive, extremely happy and thankful finally to be out of the DR and safely across the Mona Passage. That little roasted duck, even divided eight ways, still made for a great feast!

Because we preferred to eat aboard and we liked to eat well, when we would arrive in a new port we had two priorities – one was where and how we could find the local mass transit, followed by where we could provision and do it economically. We are not terribly big on convenience foods

Just one of many holiday turkeys

and, since we had only a tiny freezer, we were really limited on what we could carry in the way of perishable frozen goods. Therefore we always made a point of finding the best provisioning sources.

As you are no doubt aware, snorkeling is decent just about everywhere and is absolutely fantastic in many locations throughout the Caribbean. The northern Caribbean is no exception. We snorkeled in just about every location we visited. It's cheap and fun. Compared to scuba diving, snorkeling is a real bargain. I (David) have been a certified diver for many years and I enjoy it, but I consider scuba to be a lot of work. Snorkeling on the other hand I find to be fun and relaxing. I used to always scuba dive when we came to vacation in the islands, but once we started cruising I only used my scuba gear for working on the boat. I just had no desire to scuba when I could simply enjoy the sites from the surface and spend my time freediving.

This was another major cost-saver for us, again not because we were trying to save money, but simply because we didn't have any real urge to do it. Annie never got certified because she just never had the desire, and I don't have much interest in recreational scuba. For us this eliminated all expenses related to diving except for the occasional air fill for boat work. You are probably aware that many people who do scuba dive, do it religiously, and, unless you carry your own air compressor or a gas powered or electric hooka unit, the expenses associated with diving can be substantial.

As mentioned earlier, another area where we saved money involved commercial excursions and festivals. We still haven't quite figured this one out. We never really avoided them, we just didn't manage to get to any festivals.

When we got to the Bahamas we missed Junkanoo by a month and we heard rave revues about it. Because of our late departure from Florida, we simply had bad timing.

When we were in the Dominican Republic, a group of cruisers got together and went to the big annual merengue festival in Santo Domingo. Somehow we didn't and we're still not quite sure how we missed it, because we really did intend to go. However, in retrospect, we don't regret it since as a group they really did not fare very well. One lady had her jewelry stolen off her body by a thief in the crowd (Why she was wearing her jewelry in such a crowd, we cannot explain.) and one of the men fell victim to a pickpocket and lost his wallet with all his money and credit cards! Otherwise I guess they had a pretty good time.

While we were in the USVI the following year, we were anchored in Coral Bay on St. John when St. Thomas had their annual carnival. For whatever reason, we just couldn't get excited about it. St. Thomas is already like visiting New York City during rush hour, even when they aren't having a festival. We simply couldn't get excited about the ferry ride and then the taxi ride to downtown Charlotte Amalie to face the crowds and a large commercial extravaganza.

We did, however, get to do St. Thomas at Christmas and that was an amazing experience. We were anchored in the main harbor off Charlotte Amalie near the cruise ship docks and we dinghied in for the evening on Christmas Eve. I suppose the bulk of the tourists and cruisers had flown home for Christmas, because there were very few non-locals present. It was as if we were given an opportunity to see the local residents with their guard down. The atmosphere was truly charming and we actually felt that we were sharing a private, magic moment with them – their downtime away from the daily invasion of tourists.

We were in Culebra and also St. Martin for the hubbub of their annual regattas. Many cruisers get very excited about these regattas and some volunteer to participate by selling tickets, working concession stands, or similar activities. They are fun, but not a lot different from regattas we've been to elsewhere – just bigger and better known.

The highpoint of our festivaling however came in Antigua. We hurried along much more than is normal for us (and we actually by-passed some islands we had intended to visit) because we had been asked by our good friends, Chris and

MaryLiz aboard *Wandering Albatross*, to come to Antigua. They had applied to enter their boat in the annual Antigua Classic Yacht Regatta and they wanted us to crew. But that is another story and we'll save it for later.

Riding the bus. Public transportation lets you really get to see the country and meet some of the people.

Savannah Bay, Virgin Gorda, British Virgin Islands

Maintaining and cleaning the bottom of our boat is one of our recreational activities. As we stated earlier, one of our principal objectives when we left to go cruising was to spend as much time as we could swimming, snorkeling, and just enjoying the water. We would routinely spend a lot of time swimming and/or floating around in the water on various water toys. But if you spend too much time goofing off, often the urge to do something else will strike.

When that would happen, or, when it became apparent that the boat bottom was in need of attention, we would spend a day or two here and there diving the bottom of the boat. It gave us the opportunity to make productive use of our swimming time to catch up on our bottom maintenance. And as an added benefit, it would provide us with a thorough workout.

When we painted our bottom back in Baltimore, we used a hard-surface, red bottom paint as a base layer. Over this we placed about three coats of black ablative bottom paint. This held up quite well for about a year, but when we were in Luperón the water there (or should we say soup...) was just a bit too much for *any* bottom paint. Serious bottom cleaning had to be done about once every two or three weeks throughout the summer or things would get just ridiculously thick. This applied pretty much to every boat there. Those vessels that had been abandoned for prolonged periods of time looked like their bottom growth might extend literally all the way to the bottom of the bay! Growth on those boats became so thick that they actually sat lower in the water.

Since diving in Luperón harbor was not the most pleasant proposition, most people hired it done. I (David) did our own, in this case generally wearing scuba gear and a dive suit to protect myself as much as possible from the local sealife. The water in Luperón harbor is just teeming with tiny, squirmy, wiggly, little critters. They might be larval crabs (Land crabs are really abundant in the harbor) or maybe they're krill, I'm not certain, and some people said they were some type of shrimp. Regardless, when you dive there, they end up in your ears, in your nose, in your mouth, mustache, beard and wherever, and they squirm and wriggle until they are washed away. In addition, if you wear black, you will have literally hundreds of them stuck to your dive suit. This tends to discourage most people from swimming and diving there, and most people hired their bottom cleaning done. (And as you might have guessed, Annie opted *not* to participate in the Luperón harbor diving activities.)

In Luperón harbor, bottom cleaning was best accomplished using a large metal drywall knife which we purchased in downtown Luperón at the local *ferretería* (hardware store). Even though this tool was very effective and much faster at removing the prolific bottom growth, needless to say, it also tended to accelerate the loss of bottom paint and, by the time we left, we were in serious need of a paint job with a lot of red paint undercoat showing through. Once we left there, we never found it necessary to get that tool back out.

After we had the bottom repainted in Ponce in Puerto Rico, our maintenance went back to routine bottom scraping and we went back to doing it as a team. For normal bottom cleaning we would use the small, flexible plastic scrapers (about six inches wide) that are generally sold as fiberglass resin applicators, or the rigid plastic putty knives that they sell at *Home Depot* (We had these in one and two inch widths). We kept a variety of scrapers of varying degrees of rigidness on board. These are relatively gentle on ablative type paint and do a pretty good job of removing barnacles and most early growth. For the prop and other hard surfaces, we would use a one inch, relatively stiff metal putty knife. This combination of tools comprised our regular tool kit for routine bottom care.

When we were cleaning the bottom, and for all of our diving and snorkeling regardless of what we were doing, we always wore gloves. However, we never wore regular dive gloves. Conventional dive gloves are expensive and they snag easily and can't take a beating. The gloves that we would wear were plain old unlined leather work gloves, the type that you wear when you are working with hand tools to help prevent blisters. They protect your hands quite well and still allow some dexterity. These gloves held up remarkably well and, even when they got holes in them (Holes usually happen first at the knuckles and in the fingertips.), they could still be used for various chores until they literally fell apart. Each time when we were done diving, we would rinse them thoroughly in fresh water and let them dry in the sun.

For bottom paint we found that the regular copper-based ablative that we had when we left Baltimore, and the similar locally-made copper-based ablative paint that we had applied in Ponce, seemed to work as well as could be expected. While we were being painted at the yard in Ponce, another boat belonging to some Luperón friends was also being painted at the same time. Since that boat was aluminum, they were using a tin-based paint. Hoping to provide even better protection, the skipper added even more tin to the paint – a whole extra bottle of commercial additive to each gallon.

I was curious about the advantages of tin-based paint relative to copper. As an experiment, I borrowed one roller full of the tin-based paint and applied a patch about one foot square on one side of our stern. Once we were launched, since we cleaned our bottom manually on a very regular basis, we were able to monitor the two types of paint and compare them to each other.

The verdict? We had a one foot square patch of baby barnacles attached to that patch within a couple of weeks of being launched. Can't explain it. The rest of the boat remained relatively barnacle-free for a year or so. Bottom growth of all types, but especially barnacle growth, continued to be greatest on this little patch throughout the life of the paint job. Is this an indictment of tin-based paint? Maybe... All we can say is that, in our little test, we never noticed any advantage of the tin paint over the copper during the life of that bottom job.

There are yards throughout the islands where you can have your bottom done for you, and there are numerous places where you can do it yourself. Before we headed down to the Leewards from Puerto Rico we bought paint at the *West Marine* store in San Juan because we were able to get a good deal on an ablative paint. We eventually used it when we repainted the bottom in Antigua.

In Dutch Sint Maarten, the local *Island Water World* and *Budget Marine* stores offer bottom paints for reasonable prices. If you have a substantial amount of work to do on your boat, or if you are going to spend a significant sum of money with either of these stores while you are there, let them know up front and they will open an account for you that provides a discount off their already low prices. That, combined with their duty free status, can amount to substantial savings. Further south you can also find some good deals in Grenada, Trinidad, and Venezuela.

Even the cows enjoyed the beach in Luperón. They especially loved the kowyaking. This is the *Best Resorts* all-inclusive Luperón Beach Resort.

Where is the best place to be in the hurricane belt when it's hurricane season? The answer is really easy. The best place to be is well *away* from the hurricane belt altogether. I vote for the Great Lakes.

We were hit by Hurricane Floyd when we were in Annapolis, and again by Hurricane Isabel when we were in Baltimore. Both of these storms had lost much of their punch by the time they reached us, yet it was enough to give us a small taste of what they once were. We lucked out and fared well through both storms, but we wouldn't recommend even that experience to you if you can avoid it.

We spent eight months in Luperón harbor during the worst hurricane season in recorded history. The island of Hispaniola has its own weather, complete with fronts which result in local storms and cloudy skies, in addition to the large wintertime frontal systems which occasionally swing down from the continent, and the passing of tropical waves and storm systems during the Atlantic cyclone season. While we were there for storm season we had a couple of near misses from passing tropical systems, but nothing that was any worse than a normal wintertime front passing through. Significantly, we really had nothing even close to a direct hit. Therefore it's tough to speak intelligently about what kind of protection we actually had.

However, that said, if you look at the geography of the island of Hispaniola, the protection that Luperón offers is pretty impressive. The harbor is located on the north side of an island that is a hundred miles top to bottom and well over 200 miles east to west. According to Bruce Van Sant's book *The Gentleman's Guide to Passages South*, there are seven mountain ranges extending from east to west across this island, some of which represent the highest mountains in the Caribbean basin. We have not verified the his statistics, but we can vouch for the apparent number and size of these mountains. Pico Duarte is the tallest mountain not just in the entire Caribbean but, outside of the Andes and Rocky Mountain chains it is the tallest peak in the Western Hemisphere. Luperón harbor itself is surrounded by relatively high terrain and the harbor is lined with a forgiving shoreline of mangroves and mangrove swamp. Anchoring is good and snuggling into the mangroves offers reasonably good protection.

If a hurricane strikes the island from the east or the south, the predominant direction from which most hurricanes approach, the coastal areas and some of the internal island are vulnerable to major damage. However, because of the high mountain ranges, most of the wind and even much of the rain is likely to be absorbed by this dramatic topography well before it gets to the north coast where Luperón lies. The only direction that is significantly vulnerable is if a storm should approach from the north, and the likelihood of a hurricane traveling from north to south is pretty low. Of the locations we have seen so far, which certainly isn't much, we have not seen anything comparable to the protection offered by Luperón harbor.

Looking down on Luperón harbor.

The summer of 2008 did present some significant attacks upon the north coast of the island from a number of storms. Gustav and Faye both affected Haiti as they passed near the western end of the island, but had little effect on the DR. Hanna, moving from east to west as she passed by to the north, actually made a loopdeloop and came at the island from the north, however considerably to the west of the DR (causing some serious devastation in Haiti). And Ike swept from east to west across the north coast of the island causing much flooding and devastation, with mudslides and serious damage, again especially severe in Haiti. Personal contact with people living in Luperón through these storms informed us that, once again, Luperón was relatively unaffected even by these hits.

This is not a blanket endorsement for holing up in Luperón for storm season. But, depending upon your interests and circumstances, it may be worthy of some further research.

Boqueron, on the west end of Puerto Rico, is probably the most secure hole in Puerto Rico. It just doesn't provide much space. The south coast of Puerto Rico offers significant protection at Salinas and in the nearby bays at Jobos, but, unlike Luperón, the mountains and the protective land are to the north rather than the south, and unfortunately most storms in the Caribbean tend to travel from south to north much more frequently than in the opposite direction.

Salinas was ravaged by Hurricane Georges in 1998 with a direct hit which damaged or destroyed many vessels in the harbor. Large numbers of local boats had flocked into the bay at Salinas with futile hopes for substantial protection from the storm. Cruisers who were holed up in the mangrove swamp at nearby Jobos received no damage whatsoever and were shocked at the extent of the devastation when they returned to Salinas the following day. One more example of what happens in a storm when so many boats are present in an anchorage. Despite Puerto Rico being a relatively large island, being on the south coast greatly increases the likelihood of a direct hit, and the mangroves at Jobos are relatively small so offer less protection than would larger trees. Nevertheless, we did choose to spend a hurricane season in Salinas, complete with several precautionary runs to Jobos.

On the north side of the island the only decent harbor is at San Juan which unfortunately is too crowded and too commercial to offer much protection.

There is also reasonable protection for a few boats here and a few boats there at many locations further down island, from Benner Bay on St. Thomas, to the hurricane hole in Coral Bay on St. John, to a few spots on Tortola for shoal draft vessels. (Obviously the more shoal your draft, the better you can hunker down wherever you happen to be.) Simpson Bay Lagoon on St. Martin proved its vulnerability in 1995 with a direct hit by Hurricane Luis that resulted in the loss of over 1200 boats anchored there (an unbelievable 90+% of the boats in the lagoon), yet another example of too many eggs in one basket. Most of the problem with Simpson Bay Lagoon stems from the large number of boats, many of which are semi-abandoned, found there at any given time, along with the sheer vastness of the lagoon.

We found Jolly Harbour in Antigua to offer attractive enough hurricane protection that we chose to leave *Fidelis* there, stored on the hard, for our final summer in the Caribbean.

Other islands further south also offer some protection at certain locations. Grenada demonstrated its vulnerability with a hit from Hurricane Emily a few years ago. And Trinidad, in spite of its location 'outside' of the hurricane belt, most sailors agree, is just biding its time before it too falls victim. Although there is no sure thing, the coast of South America is probably the best choice for avoiding a hit, as is the Rio Dulce in Central America, where the likelihood of being hit is limited and you can work your way up river into the protection needed in the event of the unlikely.

These are just a few suggestions. Most veteran yachtsmen (which we clearly are not) agree that the most significant factor in a hurricane is the number of boats present at a given location.

Boats that are lost are commonly sunk by other boats which have broken loose due to poor preparation, or simply by virtue of the sheer number of vessels present in the harbor.

One thing you should understand, the insurance companies play the odds when it comes to acceptable locations for hurricane protection. And the odds have a way of eventually catching up – witness Grenada and hurricane Emily in 2005. Emily was a relative lightweight as hurricanes go, but caused major damage and destruction to the Grenada summer fleet. This tendency by the insurance carriers to put all of their eggs in one basket forces all of the insured boats into the same potentially dangerous basket. And, as mentioned above, the more boats present in a given location, the greater the likelihood of boats colliding and sinking or toppling over into one another as they sit on the hard. Combine that with the lackadaisical, 'I'm insured' attitude held by many insured boaters and the false sense of security induced by the feeling of being in a 'safe zone' and you have a sure-fire recipe for disaster.

In these marginally vulnerable areas, you are still probably better off putting your boat on the hard. Use a well-protected marina that welds their stands and straps the vessels down (as ours was in Jolly Harbour, Antigua, and many of those in Grenada now do), or a marina where they trench the keels. In Grenada, most of the boats were lost in the yards when the unsecured boats simply toppled over like dominos. Welding stands and strapping the boats to the concrete obviously is not 100% preventative, but it certainly should reduce substantially the amount of damage, especially where the protection is reasonably decent, in all but the worst hits. In Trinidad, where the holding in the harbor at Chaguaramas is said to be quite tenuous even under normal conditions, this would be an excellent course of action.

In the event of an approaching storm, since hurricane hole berths are offered up on a first-come, first-served basis, we headed for our chosen hideout at the very first suspicion that something was headed our way. We would tie ourselves into the mangroves and/or set out our anchors and 'claim our spot' well in advance of any obvious threat. We did this both in Luperón and in Jobos, near Salinas, Puerto Rico.

Probably due to its relative isolation, Jobos has a reputation for attracting very few boats. Very few locals, and few if any other boats other than hardcore cruisers tend to congregate there for storm protection. This tendency in and of itself is enough to offset any negative aspects of holing up there.

One of the acknowledged problems with hurricane holes is that they attract so many boats. Many of those boats may be owned by locals, by non-liveaboards, and even by charter companies. The boats are anchored and often inadequately prepared by people who then leave them. When the storm ultimately arrives, there is no one aboard to prevent the vessel from drifting down on other craft that are manned and properly prepared. Under storm conditions a boat, or multiple boats, drifting down on a vessel will likely overwhelm even the best preparations.

Since we had experienced two hurricanes while living up on the Chesapeake, we were somewhat familiar with how to prepare our vessel. At the point where things looked seriously threatening we would take down all of our sails, remove the solar panels, tie down the wind generator (We would wait for greater certainty of a hit before considering removal of the blades.), and get everything we could off the deck. Sometimes we would choose to leave the mainsail in place and wrap the sail and boom with a length of line, then make certain the boom was tightly secured to the boom gallows. There are good reference sources available on how to prepare for a hurricane. Read them, and heed them.

So why do so many boats stay in the Caribbean and the Bahamas during hurricane season? I think that much of it has to do with one factor. Summertime is the best time to be there. The breezes are pleasant, the water is warmer and clearer, and the crowds dwindle away. The diving in the settled waters of the relatively quiet trades is nothing short of spectacular. While we were holed up in the Salinas, Puerto Rico area, we spent the better part of a week snorkeling on the outside of the barrier islands adjacent to *Boca del Infierno*. We explored acres of pristine reef, covered with thousands of sea fans, waters that are virtually never seen by anybody during most of the year because these reefs are continually inundated by tradewind seas. We even snorkeled the *boca* itself. The Caribbean and the Bahamas are simply at their best during hurricane season. If it weren't for the hurricane risk, I'd be going around raving to everybody that they should visit the islands in the summertime.

Our experience with hurricanes is mostly by hearsay and our personal experience with hurricane holes is really limited by where we have been. We rubbed shoulders with a number of veteran Caribbean liveaboards who had personal experiences to relate, and we feel very fortunate that in our limited tropical time we avoided even any close calls. So to use an old Michiganism, we don't know squat. What we can tell you for certain is that your risk is the least if you are nowhere near the Caribbean during hurricane season. Otherwise, your best bet is to equip your boat well with good ground tackle, use your common sense, run away well in advance of even a *possible* threat, and not take any chances. Or better yet, visit the Great Lakes! Obviously we didn't allow the storm threat to stop us from living aboard in the islands during storm season, but this is a choice not to be undertaken lightly.

Sign pointing up the hill to the 'Bule Store' (which, since you can't tell from the photo, is blue) in Staniel Cay, Bahamas . There is also a 'Pink Store' which, very logically, is pink. Bahamians value common sense. Check out both stores when you are there.

Eating out and cooking and preparing meals aboard is one of the more significant expenses associated with living aboard and cruising long term. Not only where you eat, but what you eat can make a difference in your lifestyle and the cost of cruising

There are a ton of cookbooks aimed at the cruiser. Most of them deal with how to cook onboard when you have limited space and limited facilities to prepare food. They deal with using crock pots and pressure cookers, with substituting things that are 'easy to prepare' in a ship's galley for those things you might otherwise eat, and simple recipes and convenience ingredients that are supposed to change cooking aboard into something different from what is done at home in the kitchen.

But the simple fact that you have limited space and a small stove really doesn't have that much to do with what you eat. It may slow you down a bit and it may inconvenience you somewhat in the process of preparing your meals, but it really doesn't have to change how you eat or what you eat. In other words, you don't really need special cookbooks and special recipes and special foods to live and eat on board. If you like to cook your own food, then by all means do it! We did so routinely and, other than taking a little more time (Seems like we always had plenty of that while cruising.), it was no different than cooking at home. You're just doing it in a miniaturized kitchen!

We carried a couple of crock pots and a pressure cooker for the first few years we lived aboard. But we never had any urge to use them. We had no need to cook anything any faster, and we just never had any interest in relearning how to cook in order to take a step downward on the culinary ladder. We are certainly not gourmands by any stretch, and I don't have anything against cooking with crock pots and pressure cookers, but I also have never heard of either one being used in a gourmet restaurant. If I want to learn how to cook all over again, I want to learn to do it better, not faster. So we scrapped the crockpot and got rid of the pressure cooker.

We both love to eat and we like to cook. Over a period of several years of living aboard, we never changed our cooking and eating habits one bit from how we lived when we lived ashore. Our only cookbook on board *Fidelis* was a two-volume paperback copy of *The Joy of Cooking*, which we kept as a reference source and never used any more often on board the boat than we did ashore.

Turkey in the oven – plenty of room!

Indeed, from the moment we first moved aboard, each year both for Thanksgiving and for Christmas, Annie would prepare a full turkey dinner complete with mashed potatoes and gravy, stuffing, candied yams, cranberries, pies for dessert, the whole nine yards. We usually invited over at least one couple from nearby boats to share the feast and they never ceased to be amazed at her ability to pull this off with nothing more than our little three-burner *Shipmate* propane stove. There were no convenience foods used, no 'substitutes' of any kind, and no shortcuts.

We served up Thanksgiving and Christmas dinner for friends every year aboard our boat in Baltimore at the marina. And, once we got to the Caribbean we saw no reason not to continue that tradition as we cruised.

Yes, it is a little more challenging to cook with limited counter space and the size of the turkey we could prepare was limited by the size of our small oven to something less than about fifteen or sixteen pounds. But that's still plenty adequate for a number of people – and at one party we attended, along with a potluck of other delectable delights, it served at least twenty.

Large feasts are usually something of a chore to prepare even in a normal kitchen. The pies must be baked before the oven is used for the turkey. The potatoes must be boiled and mashed before the turkey comes out of the oven and the gravy is made. The yams require a separate burner and so forth. And then everything requires its counter space where it must sit while other things are prepared. Our nav station desk usually served as the staging area for any large galley production.

Living aboard a small boat is a lifestyle of on-going continual compromises. Eating shouldn't have to be. If we could not have eaten the meals we enjoy, our tenure of living aboard would have been really short. From tacos to spaghetti to pizza to beef stroganoff to casseroles and desserts, I don't think there was a single thing that we avoided eating solely because we were on a boat.

How about the barbeque grill? Most of us have one and lots of boaters use them when weekending on a short vacation cruise or when hanging out on board at the marina. But once we were out cruising, other than the occasional charter boat, we rarely saw anybody using theirs. We enjoyed using our grill at least a couple of nights a week.

Chicken and good steaks are available down in the Caribbean in many places. We grilled steaks, nice thick ones that we usually obtained from *Sam's Club* or *Costco* in Puerto Rico or from *PriceSmart* in St. Thomas. There was a little meat market adjacent to the marina complex at Red Hook in St. Thomas, that offered excellent meat at premium prices. Many cruisers swore they would not buy their steaks anywhere else. We however found the steaks at the local *Price Smart* store to be as good as any we have had anywhere.

There are other quality meat providers further down island. When good steak wasn't readily available we just bought extra chicken, which we could get virtually everywhere. Steak and hamburgers were great when just charcoal grilled with a little Montreal seasoning (we used a gas grill with lava rock 'charcoal'), and chicken we usually grilled plain or barbequed with some *Sweet Baby Ray's* barbeque sauce (our favorite) or we might jerk it. Once every few weeks we would grill shish-kabobs. We didn't use our grill just 'to avoid heating up the boat.' Our boat didn't heat up from cooking and, anyway, we spent so little time below when in the islands that that would not be an issue for us. Grilling is a special taste treat for us.

What about all that fish and seafood? Well, unfortunately hunting and gathering was not high on our list of priorities. As a result we seldom got any. Most of the places where I (David) wanted to spear, it was not legal. And most of the places where I hunted for lobster I didn't find any. I found lobster when they weren't legal and I saw tons of fish where they weren't legal to take. When we did get fresh fish from friends who had an overabundance or on those few times when we were successful at procuring our own, it was great on the grill. But mostly we usually just bought our fish, such as fresh salmon from grocery stores in Puerto Rico, and we enjoyed it either baked or grilled.

My personal experience with line fishing resulted in exactly two fish, one of which we chose to eat and enjoyed but it just wasn't a priority for us. In contrast, our good friends Bonnie and Roger aboard their catamaran, *Kokomo*, who every year travel the snowbird route from the Bahamas to New England and back, always harvest impressive amounts of seafood because it's one of their priorities. So it can definitely be done successfully.

Supposedly the best places to hook fish are in cuts and along drop-offs, situations where we were understandably more concerned with the safety of our vessel than with spending the time needed to keep a line from latching onto a rock or coral head.

One of my (David) favorite recipes to prepare in the galley was a rather simple dish of my own creation, a delicious pasta prima vera which could be thrown together in a matter of 20 minutes or so using mostly fresh ingredients that were generally available just about anywhere. I've included it here so that you can try it.

Because our style and technique of food preparation is the

Captain Doctor Dave's Pasta Prima Vera

1/4 to ½ cup of olive oil, give or take
2 Tbsp of dried basil (or a comparable amount of fresh basil)
1 heaping tablespoon of fresh, chopped garlic
1 zucchini, quartered lengthwise then cut into bite-size pieces
1 yellow banana squash, cut similar to the zucchini
1 small container of fresh, sliced mushrooms or 1 can of sliced
1 medium onion cut into bite-size wedges and separated
1whole tomato, quartered and cut into bite-size wedges
1 pound of pasta (I prefer to use linguini)
Parmesan cheese (preferably fresh grated) to taste
Salt to taste

Fill your pasta kettle with water, add a small amount of salt and a small amount of olive oil, and bring to a boil. Add your pasta and boil for seven minutes.
Once you've put your water on to boil, take the olive oil, garlic, and basil and heat it up in a large flat frying pan.
Shortly before you throw your pasta into the boiling water to cook, place the zucchini, squash, and onion in the sauté pan and start to sauté. Sauté for four minutes or so, then add the mushrooms for a minute or two, and finally the tomato for the last two minutes or so.
When your seven minutes is up, shut off the sauté pan and drain your pasta thoroughly in a colander.
Serve up a helping of pasta to each plate and cover with a large spoonful of the sauteed veggies and olive oil. Salt to taste and cover with a generous amount of the grated Parmesan cheese. This dish goes really well with a dry Italian red wine - chianti or valpolicella. Yum! Other vegetables also work in this dish.

same on board as it is at home, for the most part eating aboard does not cost us any more than it costs for us to eat the same way at home. It does however require that the galley be properly outfitted. For us it meant bringing along some of our favorite pots and pans and the necessary cooking spoons, spatulas, serving forks, and so forth. Take the time and effort to fix up your galley like it's home. Do whatever it takes and just accept the fact that, no matter what you do, your on-board galley will probably always be less comfortable and less convenient to work in than a real kitchen. So you have to do things just a tad slower – what's the hurry? Take your time and enjoy yourself. After all, you are living the dream, right?

We did carry a few special items aboard that we felt just made life a little easier. A vacuum sealer really helps preserve the quality of foods, especially meats and especially when you freeze them, when you buy them in quantity from warehouse stores. We would sprinkle our steaks with Montreal Seasoning before vacuum sealing them. It really allowed the steaks to absorb the flavor while stored. The soft, foldable rubber baking pans and sheets that are now readily available are just about the perfect solution to the storage issues encountered if you are interested in baking. They store in any available tiny space you might have and they bake very nicely. We also carried a variety of collapsible and nesting type food storage containers to help save space and to allow us to keep leftovers when necessary.

Wine is a significant part of most meals for us, so one item particularly of concern to us was a proper corkscrew. We drank boxed wine for a couple of years prior to leaving, in an attempt to develop a taste for it. That endeavor was wasted on us, as we could never get past a particularly characteristic undertaste that seemed to always permeate the boxed products. Eventually we gave up and went back to bottles. Neither the space factor or the cost nor the potential for broken glass ever became an issue for us. We just wrapped our wine bottles in bubble wrap baggies or in designated socks before storing it in the bilge and elsewhere. We can't help it. We just love to enjoy our wine and the taste got in the way.

Do you go out to eat? If you live to dine out, then your cruising budget is going to take a solid hit. Most people who like to dine out do so regularly when they are cruising. This is one part of our lifestyle that required a major change. If you like to eat in nice restaurants, that's great. But in the islands our idea of a nice restaurant required revision. One of the problems we had was that we always seemed to be disappointed when we left most restaurants. The prices that we paid seemed to be based on the ambience with little regard for the food that they served.

I (David) used to make fun of my father's philosophy when it came to eating out. He was a product of the Great Depression and when it came to food, his idea of a great restaurant was one that served large volumes of food. I would tease him and make fun of his 'The food may not be very good, but you sure get a lot of it' mentality. In the islands we found the restaurants had a variation on this theme. The food generally wasn't very good, *and* you didn't get much of it, but neither was necessary because the restaurant had a nice view. Well, you know what? Our view from the cockpit of our boat was a whole lot better, and so was our food and wine – at a fraction of the price.

As mentioned earlier, it seemed that every aspiring chef or restauranteur owned a restaurant that offered 'fine dining' just about everywhere we went. We eventually gave up on these places and gravitated toward the eating establishments where the locals ate. While we were in the Dominican Republic we both developed a taste for beans and rice, served in a number of styles, and grilled chicken was usually the meat portion of these meals (although their idea of what constitutes a particular cut of chicken was a tad unusual to us). As we traveled further down the island chain we continued to eat at the local eateries and found more variations on the beans and rice theme, and the locals also seemed to have a genuine knack for making good barbeque, both ribs and chicken. We found that most places we could generally eat a very enjoyable meal of local fare for about three dollars each, if we just looked for the local restaurants. And you know what? We found the ambience and the atmosphere and the people in these places to be the genuine real McCoy without paying a premium price for the commercialized tourist version.

When we did get the urge to go out to eat something special, it was usually for something unusual that we had a particular hankering for. How about Chinese food? It was difficult to find good Chinese in the DR and Puerto Rico. The Chinese restaurants down there served food that was slightly unusual to us and always seemed to resemble the local food in both appearance and taste. Beans and rice appeared more often and with a much more Creole flavor than they should in Chinese food. Mexican food that we found in Puerto Rico was more Tex-

Mex than what we prefer.

When we were spending hurricane season in the DR, after months without, we had a sudden urge to hit a couple of the fast food joints. Both Burger King and McDonald's are present in the larger cities. Although they seemed expensive compared to their American counterparts, they provided a pleasant change for us and, in spite of the very 'gamey' flavor of most beef in the DR, tasted *almost* like we remembered them from home.

While we were living in Luperón, for lack of anything better to do, and since Annie really enjoys baking, she decided to go into business baking goodies for the entire anchorage. She had an informal arrangement with the local yacht club restaurant to make several loaves of her super sourdough bread each week, which they used mainly for making their French toast. Also she baked goodies every week for the local flea market at the marina, to which she would take several pans of baked goods and sell them. And one morning each week she would make her cinnamon rolls which she would announce on the morning radio net. Three mornings a week of getting up at sunrise and baking – but she had a ball doing it. And if you saw the size of our tiny galley, you might wonder how she did it. But it can be done. You just need plenty of patience and don't want to be in a huge hurry when cooking in a small galley.

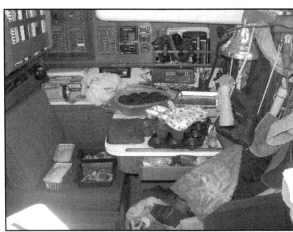

Our nav station desk cum baked goods area. Pretty congested territory on baking days. I can see two loaves of bread, two pans of cinnamon rolls, and a couple trays of muffins.

One of the 'cattle boats' seen regularly at Christmas Cove on Great St. James Island, USVI.

Captain Steve's Place in Luperón. Captain Steve is the undisputed king of the gringo entrepreneurs. Home cooked meals, laundry, wholesale goods, motorbike rental, bar and restaurant and more. He wheels and deals just about everything! In the words of a little jingle that I wrote for him, "If you can drink it, wear it, ride it, or smell it, Captain Steve's got a way that he can sell it!"

Tips for Doing the Florida to Caribbean Trip

Aim for November-December crossing from Florida
-Allow for plenty of time to get your weather window

Take your time enjoying the Bahamas and allow for getting to the southeast Bahamas by mid-April
-Once you are in the southern Bahamas, take easting when you can get it; once you've gotten it, don't give it up

Cross to the Turks and Caicos in mid to late April and take some time exploring the T&C Islands
- If you are heading down to Venezuela or Trinidad for hurricane season, speed things up *just a little* to allow for getting to the DR in early May
- Then head south to arrive in Trinidad/Venezuela by early June
- Wait for following season to come back up and explore
- If you intend to hole up in Luperón for hurricane season, you can hang out in the T&C Islands and closely watch the weather reports; at first sign of tropical activity or, by mid-June, whichever comes first, make your jump to the DR

Stay in the DR til it's safe to leave

Traversing the north coast of the Dominican Republic
Keep the breezes light (less than 10 knots) from *south of east* when traversing the north coast of the DR; use the island mass for protection
-NO northerly swell
-Watch for fish traps along the north coast of the DR

Traversing the south coast of Puerto Rico
Keep the breezes light (less than 10 knots) from *north of east* when traversing the south coast of Puerto Rico; again use the island mass for protection
- Not concerned with northerly swell; swell from east through south is occasionally a concern here
- Watch for fish traps along the south coast from Boca del Infierno eastward

ALWAYS take your time and be patient; allow for good, long weather windows
-If trades have been blowing stink, allow an extra day or so for seas to flatten out before you go

A back street in downtown Dewey, Culebra

As far as the trip from Florida to the Caribbean goes, the answer to this question is quite easy. Leave Florida earlier, take our time and stay longer in the Bahamas and in the Turks and Caicos, and arrive in the Dominican Republic later. We'll get into all of this in detail later but, for now, in a nutshell, here's the *CliffsNotes* version of what we would do.

Leave Florida somewhere between Thanksgiving and Christmas. Enjoy the Bahamas. We missed most of the Exumas and all of the Berrys and the Abacos. We missed Andros, Cat Island, Long Island, Eleuthera, Rum Cay, Conception and San Salvador, Crooked Island, Inagua, and the Jumentos, among others. That's a lot to miss. Frankly we missed just about all of the Bahamas, except those few islands we happened to stumble over.

We would probably choose to mosey our way casually along through the Exumas and the surrounding islands in order to get to the southeastern Bahamas by about mid-April, just in time for the weather to start settling down a little more. In late April or early May we would have taken off for the Turks and Caicos and cruised there for a few weeks in May while closely monitoring the weather. At the first sign of a tropical disturbance headed our way, or by mid-June, whichever came first, we would scoot across to Luperón and hole up for the summer.

If your boat is insured and you have to follow the dictates of your gambling buddies at the insurance company whose job it is to play the odds and consequently force you to go where it's "safe," then you could skip down to the DR, either Luperón or *Ocean World*, in early May to rest up and refuel, then scoot on down to Trinidad, Grenada, or Venezuela to arrive by early June.

With regard to our other cruising choices, it's difficult to consider how to cruise differently. Since every boat and every situation is essentially a compromise, one must make a choice among which negatives to choose to live with and what ones to change.

A bigger boat is more comfortable and obviously offers

much more space, usually a better ride, more speed, and may even have an edge when it comes to safety. But it also comes with much more expense, both in initial purchase price and in maintenance costs. In other words, regardless of the size or type of vessel, a cruising boat is always a package of compromises.

We would definitely have loved to have the larger master stateroom and berth of a larger boat or especially of a larger center cockpit vessel. A larger galley, with nice stone or Corian countertops, would have been great, but only as a convenience. We certainly could not have done much more elaborate cooking than what we did.

One thing that I (David) always missed on our boat was a second stateroom. It would have been wonderful to have friends and/or relatives come to visit us and have them be able to have a room all their own. We rarely had any visitors while we were cruising, partly because we didn't have any designated 'visitor space.' But I think much of the reason we didn't get a boat with space for visitors had a lot to do with the fact that we tend to be fairly private with our lives. In addition, we were always amazed at the difficulties encountered by cruising friends of ours who did invite visitors and then had to deal with the often complex logistics of just getting and keeping their friends aboard. First it requires the right weather for the visit with a desirable weather window to allow them to get to the right harbor; dinghying their visitors from shore to the boat and back, loading all of that usually excessive luggage and other unnecessary items into the dinghy and then finding room for it all on the boat. Then there is the need for accommodating the luxurious water and energy usage habits of people who have lived a life ashore with no concern for how much of either resource they use, all done while taking them out for several days of blissful relaxation in just the right anchorage while trying to make certain that the engine operates, the refrigeration works, the dinghy runs, the sails don't self-destruct, and the head continues to function.

There are many times we wished we had a shallower draft. Our nominal six foot draft (actually much closer to seven foot in real life) was a bit excessive for many of the spots we wanted to get to, especially on the banks of the Bahamas and the Turks and Caicos. But it was more than welcome when we were in deep water and the wind piped up, and was a wonderful feature whenever we were on a longer passage. And we always wished we had a drier bilge.

On the CSY 37 we have a cockpit sole hatch cover that allows access to the engine – I mean complete and almost totally unrestricted access to the engine, a veritable godsend should the need arise. However, the downside is that water coming into the cockpit (usually through the cockpit scuppers themselves, whenever we heel over) easily drains into the engine compartment and into the bilge. Even when it rains, some water gets into the bilge. When we take our showers in the cockpit, water gets into the bilge. When you wash down the decks..... and so on and so forth. Yes, every piece of every boat is a compromise. Which ones did you (or will you) choose?

We found it necessary to raise our waterline a few inches before we left the Chesapeake. In retrospect we should have raised it several inches. The more or less continuous wind chop, often several inches high in a Caribbean anchorage, is much more constant than that encountered in the sheltered anchorages enjoyed when coastal cruising or when sitting in a slip tied to a dock. We could have avoided some paint issues if we had just anticipated this apparently insignificant difference.

So make the right choices where they are easy and where they are important to you. Once you've made the choices and it's too late to change them, forget about them. Move on to those things that are important. But most of all, get going.

At boat shows I end every seminar that I do by telling my attendees that you can always spend more money, and you can always find more things to do to get your boat ready to go. But frankly, you don't really need to do anything except get away from the dock. Once you are away from the dock, you'll figure out what's important. And once you're away from the dock, staying away from the dock will become so important that you'll find a way to fix the stuff that really and truly *is* important.

Looking out from the bay in Boqueron, Puerto Rico

I bring this up here only because it is an issue that I have not seen addressed in any other book or publication on cruising. It is a topic that is seldom discussed among cruisers. The cruising life tends to be carefree and laid back and when you are out there there is a tendency to not want to think about the darker side of things. But the truth is that the cruising community is quite representative of all people and all lifestyles. Although you certainly don't want to dwell on it, you must constantly be aware that some of those people and their lifestyles might tend to fall into the unsavory category.

In our four years of living aboard and cruising in the Caribbean, I (David) occasionally performed veterinary services for other cruisers and at times for locals alike. Never during that time did anyone ever inquire as to my credentials or ask me for any form of identification or licensing information. And frankly I would have been surprised if they had, such being the nature of those in the cruising community. But it is something that really needs to be considered when you are asked by a 'fellow cruiser' to shell out several hundred or even several thousand dollars for 'expert' attention to your boat, your engine, your outboard, or whatever else might be under consideration.

Nobody likes a party pooper and we don't want to rain on your beach party, but the naked truth is that when you are out cruising, you are who you say you are. The corollary to that statement is, of course, that you can be anybody that you want to be – and so can the other guy. We encountered people who were out there cruising under false names. We didn't feel they were dishonest. They were just sort of 'starting over' with their new life and were enjoying a new identity. But we also encountered people who had taken it to the next level and were dishonest, and some who were downright treacherous. A lot of trusting individuals were taken in by these people.

One boat developed a reputation for hitting the local computer cafes and restaurants and offering to 'upgrade' or introduce new equipment and services in exchange for free meals. We knew of at least three different locations where they had visited. Each time when they left, they left such a wake of computer problems behind that the restaurant owners had to hire outside experts to come in and attempt to undo the damage. One café owner that we talked to spent over $10,000 for the 'expertise' of this person and then subsequently the cost of undoing the damage. It was our impression from talking with the victims of this flim-flam that the problems left behind may even have been of an intentional, malicious nature. Last thing we knew, these 'friends' of ours were still out there cruising and probably still pulling the same scam.

BEWARE: When you are out there cruising, you can be whoever you want to be. Just remember, so can the other guy. When money and/or items of value are at stake, KNOW who you are dealing with. If you aren't absolute certain, then find out!!!

Another couple we encountered in the Dominican Republic had been living aboard there for years. They left a year or more after we passed through, evidently by obtaining a boat whose owner had hired them to deliver that boat to another island as delivery captain and crew. The alleged delivery turned into a cruise around the Caribbean after which they charged the owner for their time. The exorbitant delivery charge ended up being contested in court and they were evidently awarded ownership of the boat in lieu of payment. While we were in the DR this same person was a self-proclaimed 'diesel mechanic' and reportedly irreparably damaged a number of engines that he worked on and/or overhauled. One couple we knew chose to sail home to Canada without a functioning engine rather than allow themselves to be taken in any longer by any more of his work. We ourselves were familiar with at least two cases where he did seriously substandard work.

Don't let yourself fall victim to this type of fraud. Check around. Even the nicest people are not necessarily who they say they are and some are not necessarily on the up and up. Living aboard a boat and cruising is a relatively inexpensive lifestyle, but it is not free. For those of us who choose to do it on a small budget or a meager income, it requires self control and care. For those who do it on no budget and who have little or no income or who live beyond their means, the money must come from somewhere, and some of them will resort to any means to stay out there.

Fidelis at anchor in Simpson Bay Lagoon, St. Martin

Yes, we rented a scooter (but not a motor*bike*). And yes, one of us got injured.

PART TWO

THE TRIP

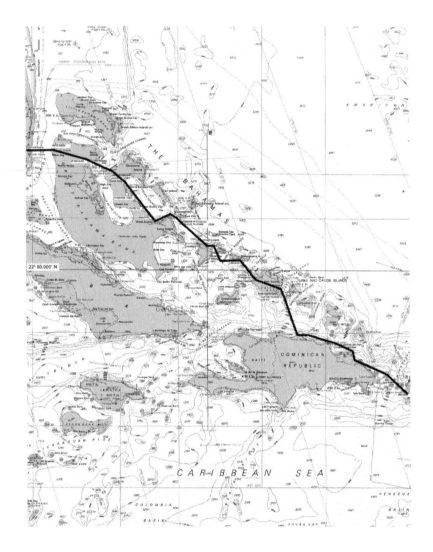

Florida to Puerto Rico – *Fidelis'* route to windward

It was time to go. More than three years in Baltimore living aboard '*Fidelis*' year-around was enough. What had originally started out as a six-month rest stop for purposes of seeing and experiencing a new city while we gave a shot in the arm to our cruising kitty had, much to our chagrin, turned into almost four years. David had a working arrangement with a nearby veterinary hospital. He had been hired on temporarily but had really enjoyed the convenience of a short three-block walk to work each day while working only four days a week. In addition, his employers had become somewhat dependent upon his talents as a veterinarian cum hospital manager. Annie, on the other hand, had assumed the multiple roles of dockmaster and marina manager at *HarborView Marina* where she was experiencing unprecedented success to the point where she was finding it difficult to break the ties.

Back in 1996 we had bought *Fidelis* in Tortola in the BVI – sort of a souvenir of one of our combination camping and charter boat trips. It was an unexpected purchase and not a particularly wise move at the time (or any other time for that matter). Impulse purchases are never a good idea, but whims border on the insane when they measure in the thousands of dollars, even though for the most part we had lucked out and not gotten burned. Annie, with a hired captain, eventually delivered the boat from the Caribbean to the Chesapeake, where a truck picked it up and carried it on to Michigan. We spent the next two years refurbishing the boat and having the engine overhauled, before leaving the Great Lakes in July of 1999 to head across the Erie Canal, down the Hudson River through New York Harbor and on down the east coast to Chesapeake Bay.

We had grown to love Baltimore and our particular location within it. Driving was only necessary for those major provisioning trips and special events. We resided only a ten-minute walk from the hustle and bustle of the inner harbor. The parade of tall ships, over a hundred of them at once from all over the world, arrived while we were there. Events and shows and diversions were happening every weekend throughout the year.

Restaurants, shops, and activities abounded. An enjoyable urban-style old-office-building-cum-movie-theater complex was a pleasant one mile walk uptown from us. The Ravens brought home a Super Bowl victory our first year there with all of the associated festivities. We walked over to *Camden Yard* and attended Orioles baseball games on a regular basis and enjoyed our metropolitan surroundings to the max. We loved it dearly and we enthusiastically recommend Baltimore and its Inner Harbor as a requisite stop for those cruisers doing the east coast and the ICW. It was truly difficult to pull up stakes and leave.

Besides our fondness for Baltimore we had developed an interest in the Bay. Chesapeake Bay has to have more gunkholes per square mile of water than any comparable body of water on the planet. Coming to the Chesapeake was an awakening of sorts for us. Up on southern Lake Huron, government-constructed harbors are placed at roughly thirty-mile intervals along a glacial coastline that could not have been more lacking in nooks and crannies if it had been bulldozed. Coming from our neighborhood on Saginaw Bay we had to cruise nearly 200 miles to the North Channel and Georgian Bay to reach an area where short daysails and sheltered anchorages were plentiful – beautiful scenery with clear but cold water and often cool, cloudy weather. It was beautiful but just too chilly to be our cup of tea. On the Chesapeake, even with our nearly seven-foot draft, weekend jaunts and the occasional several days of vacation allowed us to experience a variety of anchorages within just daysail distance. It was a real treat being able to leave our marina in Baltimore in mid-afternoon and drop the hook in a protected cove well before dark. We enjoyed the Chesapeake tremendously, yet probably not as much as we would have had our thoughts and dreams not been constantly wandering much further to the south.

The weather was what ultimately made the decision easy. The first six months in Baltimore when with trepidation we experienced our first winter of living aboard had surprisingly become the proverbial piece of cake – chilly nights, balmy days, no snow, and just the occasional brushing of cool winds from a

Living the dream in Baltimore. It was time to leave.

passing front. At the time we hadn't a clue what an exceptional winter it really was. The harsh reality of the following two winters brought us back to our senses. Record-setting cold and record-breaking snow in back to back winters hit us with a sledgehammer blow of reality.

In our previous life when we were back in Michigan, shoulders to the grindstone mingled with occasional weekend sailing, we had always laughed at those hardy souls who felt bold enough to serve themselves up "bubbled-on-ice" for an endless Michigan winter on Lake Huron. Yet here we were doing the same thing under conditions that were just as severe as any Michigan winter that we had ever known. Baltimore winters however did have two saving graces not found in Michigan. Sunshine came through on a regular basis to brighten up many a winter's day, a rarity reserved for only a handful of days in Michigan's perpetual darkness. Between that and the relative shortness of a Maryland winter – December to March beat Michigan's November to May winters hands down (but that was only in November, April, and May) – a Chesapeake Bay winter was infinitely more tolerable than that spent on the periphery of the Great White North.

So we bid a fond adieu to Baltimore and the Chesapeake. After years of working on the boat, preparing and fitting out and improving followed by more of the same, one morning in August we headed east out of the Patapsco River and hung a right. We were finally off. We anchored out at a few places on our way down the bay – a whole month or so in Annapolis for the boat show and some socializing with our sailing friends, the South River, Solomons, Deltaville. Finally we cruised through Hampton Roads and into Norfolk, Virginia where a minor leak in the plastic capillary tube of our oil pressure gauge mortally wounded our old but rebuilt Perkins engine. The layover resulted in one of those classic 'series of unfortunate events' which very nearly snuffed out our longstanding dream of cruising the Caribbean. The tale of the ensuing incompetent repair work by a facility in Portsmouth would make a horror story of its own and will not be detailed here. Suffice it to say that many weeks and many, many thousands of dollars later we were finally ready to continue our southbound odyssey.

A few days after Thanksgiving, our sanity was beginning to return and *Fidelis* was finally ready to continue south. After our third attempt at leaving the incompetence of the Portsmouth diesel shop behind us, we had inadvertently found ourselves rescued by a repair facility in Great Bridge, Virginia, and will forever be grateful for

Star Island, Miami Beach

having stumbled across a company steeped in knowledgeable, professional technicians. With the iciness of winter breathing down our necks we continued down the ICW.

Christmas was spent dodging snowflakes in New Smyrna, Florida as we did some minor repairs, working some bugs out of our newly installed engine. With our nearly seven foot draft, we continued our personal dredging of the ICW and arrived in Melbourne, Florida in early January. We had reservations at a marina in Melbourne where we left the boat for about a month while we tied up some final loose ends prior to our planned Gulf Stream crossing. Once that layover was behind us, we continued on south toward Miami, heading 'down the outside' from Fort Pierce to Lake Worth, and again from there to government cut in Miami. Finally, in Miami we anchored for nearly three weeks off Miami Beach while we waited what seemed a virtual eternity for a weather window. At last it was time for our long-anticipated Gulf Stream crossing.

Because crossing the Gulf Stream is a major event for most Bahamas cruisers and we had been hearing about it since long before our Chesapeake departure, we were naturally concerned about doing it right. We took every opportunity to pick the brains of those more experienced than we. Anchored off Hibiscus Island, we attended a Super Bowl party aboard a small trawler where we discussed things with some other 'newbies' and made plans for staying in touch by radio. A weather window seemed to be approaching and we didn't want to miss it.

We listened to both NOAA weather on the VHF and Chris Parker's Caribbean Weather service on the HF radio. Things seemed to be coming together and a useable weather window appeared imminent. The day before our expected crossing we weighed anchor and headed off toward Biscayne Bay and the protection of an anchorage just outside of Hurricane Harbor. The night before our expected departure we were on the VHF talking with some of the veterans of previous crossings. A couple of vessels had done it two or three times, while one boat had made the passage five times before. They suggested we just follow them out and they would hold our hand to get us started.

The next morning arrived with that post-frontal vividness and color and at daybreak, with our Sea Tiger 555 manual windlass, we were popping our *Delta* anchor out of the sandy bottom in twelve feet of water and following the pack out of the anchorage as we headed out through Biscayne Channel. We closely monitored our electronic charts and our fathometer as we cautiously motored through and around the unfamiliar shoals. The day had dawned clear and bright with a very light breeze blowing from the east. As we motored easterly by slightly southeast we raised our mainsail in a routine that would become so familiar on the trip upwind to the islands – an effort to gain a little stability and possibly pick up a fraction of a knot as we slowly but steadily motored upwind.

We had gotten several miles behind us when we began to hear some chatter on the VHF. The light easterly breeze was not settling down at all and, if anything, may have built up just a tad. The going had become lumpy and a little on the uncomfortable side. People were complaining and some had decided to turn back. Our acquaintances on the trawler found the going too unpleasant and packed it in. Even the veteran boats were turning back. About a third of the way across we got a call from the five time crossing veterans telling us they were heading back with hopes of trying again tomorrow. Annie and I looked at each other. Here we were on a beautiful, sunny day making a crossing that we would have considered pretty mild back home on Lake Huron where the wind always blows from the wrong quarter. Granted it was the Gulf Stream, but we already had one-third of the trip behind us. Another twenty miles and we should begin to enjoy a little lee from the Great Bahama Bank. We decided to find the most comfortable speed and angle of attack on the two foot chop and just tough it out. The weather was holding steady with no sign of deteriorating and the ride was not dangerous to us or harmful to the boat in any way. The decision was made to continue and we passed the word along to our friends on the

VHF. We were committed.

A few hours later as we made our approach to Bimini, we again began to hear voices on the VHF. Boats were evidently standing by, waiting to go into the harbor at Alice Town. We heard the boat name *Dragonfly* and at the time did not give it much thought. It wasn't until later that we found it was the same *Dragonfly* with whom we had shared our slip space at *HarborView Marina* in Baltimore the previous winter. Fred and Joyce, whom we had barely had the time to meet when we lived next door to them in our workaday world of Baltimore, became very good friends as we subsequently worked our way down to Nassau and the Exumas.

A slight smudge on the horizon grew into the Bimini islands well before the easterly chop showed any inclination toward abating, and we finally found ourselves standing off North Bimini. With our nearly seven foot draft, we opted to wait for the tide while we inquired on the VHF for someone with local knowledge to hopefully help guide us in. A very cordial local dive boat with a similar depth requirement responded and volunteered their assistance, leading us through the serpentine channel entrance where we not surprisingly bumped a couple of times. Eventually we tucked in at Weech's Marina in Alice Town at about 2:30 PM and put our first Gulf Stream crossing behind us.

"Houseboats" in La Parguera, Puerto Rico

We originally had intended to take the offshore route on this trip. Our logic was that we would just bite the bullet, get it over with, and be in the Caribbean. We had both done some offshore trips, but frankly neither one of us relishes those trips. The offshore route, leaving from Beaufort, North Carolina and heading east toward Bermuda, then turning south and heading for the islands – essentially the *Caribbean 1500* route – is the standard itinerary for leaving from the Atlantic coast. We are not big joiners or group particpators, so the *1500* as an event held little appeal for us. We had friends who had made the trip with the *1500* over the years and we were not impressed by the organization's attention to the weather. Because of the regimented planning of the event, they are not sufficiently flexible to allow taking advantage of weather opportunities. In our experience, a weather window that opens a day or two prior to the event or a few days after their scheduled departure could often make a world of difference in the quality of the trip. They just don't have that kind of flexibility.

After making our decision to do the offshore trip and after fitting our boat with a *Monitor* windvane, we had begun to have some second thoughts. We didn't know how long we were going to be gone or how far we were going to go. We had discussed possibly cruising the coast of South America and/or the Orinoco River, or perhaps crossing the Atlantic to the Med, and we had even offhandedly discussed the possibility of traversing the Panama Canal and heading across the Pacific. Since we had never been to the Bahamas we began to think, what if we miss the Bahamas? We might not get that chance again. Our plans started to slowly evolve. During the last year or so of planning, we got Bruce Van Sant's book *The Gentleman's Guide to Passages South* and we did a little research. We went and saw Bruce speak at a local cruiser's gam, and we decided the Bahamas was worth a visit. Eventually the tide turned and we began to gird ourselves for the challenge of taking on the 'thorny path.'

We cannot be enthusiastic enough in recommending this

book. Without sounding like one of those Bruce Van Sant worshipers that we occasionally encountered on our trip, it is difficult to sufficiently stress the importance of his *Gentleman's Guide*. For those who are relatively new to the Bahamas or to island sailing, his advice is priceless. Information on island effects, cape effects, local weather systems, and staging out prior to a passage; advice on obtaining your weather information and interpreting it; discussions about being self sufficient in your decisions and avoiding the pack mentality, along with suggested routes for making your way south and east through the Bahamas, and possible jumping off points for making your passage from the southern Bahamas to the Dominican Republic – it's all there along with very passable cruising guide information for the DR, Puerto Rico, and the Spanish Virgins. Our book rapidly wore out and began to self-destruct and we graduated to a new copy of an updated revision. In our preparations for departure and in our frequent references to it while coming down island, we used it to the point where I eventually jokingly referred to the entire island hopping, upwind cruising, thorny path rigamarole as "Brucin' it." We were Brucin' our way to the islands.

For those of you who are seasoned sailors and think that "I'll just do it my way," the book contains what should be some very convincing arguments against trying to make your jump from the southern Bahamas directly to the Virgin Islands or Puerto Rico. If you have chosen to visit the Bahamas, then you have already swapped away your chance to do the *Caribbean 1500*-style offshore *sailing* trip. You could just as easily consider taking the scenic route down through the Windward Passage and along the south coast of Hispaniola, but I wouldn't recommend that either. Of course, you can still do it your way. After all, it is your boat. It just won't be much *fun*.

Once you are in the Bahamas, you need to give up on the idea that the thorny path is a *sailing* trip at all, and understand that it is a motoring trip, pure and simple, with an objective of getting to the Caribbean, at which point you will then be able to enjoy all the sailing your little heart might desire. The idea of the book is to take this potentially miserable upwind trip and, by applying a number of island hopping principals, make it not only tolerable, but actually *fun*!

If you have thoughts of sailing to the Caribbean in the same way as the sailors of old, then you need to understand that they weren't stupid, and their boats weren't that efficient. They made the trip by sailing *down*wind, not by beating their way *up*wind. It's extremely unlikely that you will get a weather window anywhere near sufficiently long enough to allow making a 500 mile upwind slog without getting the crap beat out of you and your boat (unless you happen to own a megayacht, in which case you won't be aboard for the trip anyway – your flunkies will be doing all the work, right?) We frequently heard these hardy individuals talking with Chris Parker on the HF weather net. At least two different boats that we heard had lost a rudder trying to make this trip. Others made it, but were obviously not enjoying the trip as they pleaded to Chris for more decent conditions to develop.

In his book Bruce does have a tendency to rant and rave and be sarcastic in his writing style (not unlike his normal, cantankerous personality when you listen to him in person), but don't let his style and his caustic commentary distract you from the valuable information that he presents. Those times that we were most uncomfortable were generally a result of 'taking a shot at it,' or otherwise not having the patience to wait it out. Frankly, without sounding too overzealous I would go so far as to say that the more strictly you follow his advice, the less likely it is that you will find yourself in that miserable, uncomfortable situation of getting beaten up. So read the book, then reread it – and then, maybe combining it with a little of your own common sense, pay attention to what it tells you. Enough said.

Preparing to leave, we obtained all of the pertinent electronic charts that we could find that were compatible with our *Cap'n* computer navigation program. We also bought three small, hand-held *Garmin* GPS units with NMEA cords to connect to our laptops which would allow us to navigate by computer. We carried *MapQuest* paper chartbooks for the ICW and coastal Florida and similar chartbooks for the Bahamas and for the Virgin Islands.

We didn't find out until we got to Bimini, but for the Bahamas the hands-down best charts available are those published by Monty and Sara Lewis as the *Explorer Charts* (explorercharts.com). They are available as a number of waterproof chartbooks for the different Bahamas regions: the Abacos, the Exumas, and the out islands. The *Explorer Charts* are unequivocally the best charts that we have ever used. We strongly recommend them to anybody visiting or even just passing through the Bahamas.

Another set of books that we found to be handy are those by author Steve Pavlidis. His guides contain charts that he has produced himself, using his own hydrographic surveys. They are not sketch charts. He takes official government charts and, using his own surveys, superimposes additional detail far beyond what the government charts contain, making them much more valuable to shallow-water cruisers, especially worthwhile in cuts, passages, and anchorages. This results in chart detail that often is not available anywhere else. His charts and the *Explorer Charts* provide considerable overlap, but this redundancy often provides a useful comparison. In addition, Pavlidis' charts for the Turks and Caicos and the north coast of the Dominican Republic are the only detailed charts available. Get his *The Exuma Guide* and also his cruising guide to *The Southern Bahamas* (which now apparently contains his guide to the Turks and Caicos) and, along with the *Explorer* chartbooks, you should be all set for this portion of the trip. In addition, all of the above are also available on disk.

For the Turks and Caicos and the Dominican Republic there are some decent relatively small scale charts available from *Wavy Line.* They serve adequately as sailing or coastal charts for your longer passages. Other than those provided by Pavlidis, we were never able to find any detailed large scale charts for these areas.

Once you reach the Caribbean, the *Caribbean Yachting*

Charts (*CYC* charts) are the acknowledged popular standard for the cruising sailor, although the older Donald Street charts, available from *Imray-Iolaire* are also excellent. Again, a different set of charts gives you a 'second opinion' of sorts, never a wasted effort. Additionally, all of the above mentioned charts are also available in electronic form.

Besides the above charts, you may want to have various cruising guides aboard. There are other guides to the Bahamas besides those by Steve Pavlidis. And once you get to the Caribbean, there are guides to the Virgin Islands, guides to the Leeward and Windward Islands, Trinidad/Tobago, the ABC's, Cuba, the Western Caribbean and elsewhere written by Nancy Scott, Chris Doyle, Steve Pavlidis, Nigel Calder, and others. For the most part, choices in cruising guides are personal and depend upon personal preference. In some areas they are merely descriptions of where to eat, drink, shop, and party, while for other areas they may be a valuable adjunct to your coastal cruising charts. Your best bet is to ask around among veteran cruisers of those areas you intend to visit.

Chalk's Airline plane landing at Bimini. Until going out of business in 2007, they were the oldest continuously operating airline in the world.

Bow riding across the Great Bahama Bank.

We had intended to take our time and enjoy the Bahamas, but we somehow were beginning to feel a time squeeze. Earlier we had felt the squeeze from our extended repair stopover in Virginia and then again with both the business stay in Melbourne, Florida and the lengthy wait for weather in Miami. We knew all along that, given our circumstances, our original desire to make a late-December Gulf Stream crossing was unrealistic. Once we left Miami, we thought, "This is it. We're finally on our way."

It was in Bimini as we were evaluating our upcoming trip, that we discovered the amazing difference between the *Explorer* charts and the chartbook that we had brought. Fortunately we were able to obtain a full set of three *Explorer* chartbooks at the little hardware store adjacent to the marina and we were ready to roll.

We spent three days waiting for a satisfactory weather opportunity for crossing the Great Bahama Bank. When it came time to leave Alice Town, we left in the company of four other boats, rounding the south point of South Bimini and the wreck of the *Sapona*. Since our draft required a minimum of eight feet of water, we chose to follow the deeper draft route, and since the others departing for Nassau had also elected to take that route, we teamed up and formed a small fleet – *Dragonfly*, *GeWil*, *Breezy8*, *Sea Lion*, and *Fidelis*. We left in mid-morning, giving the sun adequate time to rise high enough to improve bottom visibility on the banks. As one of the slower boats and the deepest keeled, we positioned *Fidelis* in the rear guard. That way, if somebody should stumble across an unexpected shoal, hopefully we would get advance warning. Our plan was to stop at Russell Light, located at the junction of the Bank and the Northwest Channel, a protrusion off the Tongue of the Ocean. When the weather cooperates, this is standard procedure for those making the Bimini to Nassau run with an overnight stop. As we approached Russell Light, the light was on, but suddenly it went dark and, in typical Bahamas fashion, as far as we could tell, it never came back on all night long. About two miles past the light, we dropped the hook in twelve feet of water. This was a totally foreign experience for us, as we sat drinking a late evening sundowner while sitting out in what appeared to be literally the middle of the ocean with virtually no land in sight. It left us with a bit of an eerie feeling.

Next morning we weighed anchor and were off to New Providence. We entered Nassau Harbour in the late afternoon and dropped the hook just a quarter mile before the first bridge, on the south side just off the BASRA station. (For security reasons, avoid being in the first tier of boats nearest the shoreline.) Holding in Nassau Harbour is notoriously poor. Much of the bottom has patchy clods of vegetation that tend to pull loose when you latch onto them – a slight change in wind direction or velocity may be all it takes to break loose a then-fouled anchor. This happened to us on two separate occasions while anchored for our three week stay in Nassau. Our old *Delta* anchor, which we had grown so fond of while sailing on the Great Lakes and Chesapeake Bay, had failed to hold. Dragging due to a cloddy bottom fouling the anchor had happened to us several years earlier up on Lake Michigan. We wrote this experience off once again, as 'pilot error.'

Since Annie found it necessary to make a business trip back to the States for three weeks, we had to put our trip on hold while David held down the fort in Nassau. During the stay, computer problems necessitated some serious repair work on our old HP laptop and, because of our uncertainty as to the reliability of the unit, just to be safe Annie brought back a new replacement laptop from the States. The old HP was relegated to backup status. At that point we were finally ready to begin our cruising life for keeps – no more screwing around. Nonetheless, the three week hiatus in Nassau had only served to add fuel to our gnawing sensation of being behind.

At this point we should mention the rock. When we got to Nassau it was not marked. It had just been hit by and nearly sunk a virtually brand new Manta catamaran. We had noticed the cat sitting on the hard behind the BASRA station, just ashore of where we were anchored. Evidently there was a big tadoo over the whole incident with the catamaran owners suing the manufacturer (the supposedly watertight bulkheads had proven to not be so watertight).

Anyway, the Nassau authorities were placing a lighted marker next to the rock while we were there. The marker may or may not still be there when you go, the rock undoubtedly will be. Don't hit it. The rock is huge – maybe the size of a tractor trailer (you can see it well from the bridge above) – and lies just deep enough to generally not disturb the water's surface. It lies just to the east of the first bridge crossing over to *Atlantis*, on the south side of the channel, just outside of the entrance to a couple of the marinas. Don't challenge it. If you hit it, it will no doubt win the battle.

ALLENS CAY – After nearly a month in Nassau, we were ready to hustle off to Buffalo; or in this case, the Exuma islands. We were catching the latter portion of a weather window, but we only had a daysail to do – across the Yellow Banks to Allens Cay, where we intended to hole up an wait out an approaching cold front. We were still green about those things, but we lucked out. Had we gotten shut out of the anchorage at Allens Cay, we might have been in trouble. We didn't have a contingency plan and it would have been difficult to come up with adequate protection from what turned out to be an impressive front – under the circumstances, a relatively benign learning experience. (By the way, wherever you go, the word *cay* is pronounced "key" as you head down island, not "kay." You will hear a lot of people mispronounce it. Try to avoid the temptation of joining them.)

Allens Cay was our first experience using the Bahamian moor. We had our favored 45 pound *Delta* anchor on the starboard bowroller, and our FX-37 *Fortress* deployed on the portside roller. Since we were nearly the last arrival of the day at what is a relatively small anchorage, we were relegated to a less favorable spot. In spite of this, we seemed to be reasonably well protected. We dropped our *Fortress* in sand off the port bow, set it, then took the *Delta* off in another direction and supposedly set it also. Things felt reasonably secure with the front approaching, carrying with it winds in the 30 to 40 knot range.

For a good twenty-four hours we rocked and rolled in what felt like a giant *Maytag*. Several times during the blow I commented to Annie about how secure things felt with the limited swinging circle of two anchors. As the winds clocked their way around, I went on deck several times to check the chains and snubbers and make certain all was well. We were riding it out in fine fashion.

The weather eventually settled and we made preparations for our departure. Only upon retrieving the anchors did we become aware that the *Delta* was lying on its side on the bottom – like a piece of trash in the middle of a parking lot. Certainly not the anchor's fault – I'm sure I probably placed it in a relatively scoured area where any holding was negligible. It did cause us some second thoughts however on all of the possibly misplaced confidence we had had in that anchor and in our newly acquired technique. On the other hand, the occasion was a definite feather in its cap for the *Fortress*.

WARDERICK WELLS CAY – As mentioned earlier, because of our deep draft our choice of anchorages was limited most places we visited in the Bahamas. We considered our alternatives for heading south from Allens Cay. We had looked at Norman Island, but our draft would not allow us access to the more desirable pond anchorage. We had planned on getting in as close as we

Warderick Wells Cay, Bahamas

could to the protected anchorage at Norman but knew it would be difficult with our draft. However, in the morning, Fred and Joyce on *Dragonfly*, who were further along the way, called us on the single sideband radio and let us know that they had placed us on the waiting list the previous day for a mooring at the park. As we were approaching Norman, the park officials called *"Fidelis"* on the VHF to let us know that our name had come up. So it was on to Warderick Wells and Exuma Park, the Bahamian national park.

Warderick Wells, with its palm trees, turquoise water, and sandy beaches is one of the most classic looking tropical scenes we have seen – the ultimate in idyllic and very photogenic. A dozen or so moorings are available for a modest fee. If you care to spend a day doing some manual labor, you can rent yourself out to the park managers in exchange for a free mooring. Annie and I planned a two-day stay and since one of us was going to be gone why not both? So we spent a day with both of us working out on one of the walkways of this desert island moving rocks to build a small causeway for the walking trail. When our day ended and it was time to cash in for our free two days of mooring, only then did anybody bother to tell us that just one person could qualify per day from any particular vessel, so the park in effect got a day of free slave labor from us. The work was not exactly grueling but it certainly was not what we would otherwise have chosen to do with our time. Just a little word of advice in case you have thoughts along similar lines.

The snorkeling was beautiful at Warderick Wells. Wintertime water temperatures in the Bahamas are not particularly inviting, so a wet suit helps to make things more tolerable. In spite of a shorty wetsuit, I found myself limited to not much more than half an hour of dive time. Annie, in her lycra diveskin, was cold even sooner.

STANIEL CAY and THE MAJORS – From Warderick Wells we continued our trip down the inside of the Exuma chain heading for Staniel Cay. Our original anchorage of choice, just off the marina at Sampson Cay, was not as protected as we had

115

Big Rock Cut

hoped and yet had attracted just a little more company than we were seeking. We jumped in our dinghy and went out to explore the cut connecting our anchorage with the one between the Majors. The current was flowing too strong for us to attempt what appeared to be some close-quarter navigation on our own with just our computer. However, with the help of one of our Bimini cohorts guiding us in his dinghy, we made it through cleanly and dropped the hook between Big Majors and Little Majors Spot.

Another front came through while we were anchored here, so we ended up staying on for four days. During that time Annie and I considered and reconsidered how to carry on from here. We were enjoying the Exumas and enjoying our time spent with our newfound friends that had crossed from Miami with us. We had indulged in music making and small get-togethers as we socialized our way this far down, but they were about to head off in their own pursuits and we felt it was time for us to do the same. In typical cruiser fashion we enjoyed a St. Patrick's Day potluck on the beach with other cruisers where Annie contributed a large pot of corned beef and cabbage. However, at the same time we were feeling the time crunch from our late departure from Miami and our extended Nassau stay.

We were green at this. Island hopping of this nature was new to us. We knew we had to pass through one of the cuts in order to get out into Exuma Sound. At some point soon our deep draft was going to become more and more of a factor as we headed south on the banks. Sometime before Cave Cay we were going to have to make the jump to 'the outside' before we ran out of water.

We had heard about the cuts from other cruisers, about the mistake of trying to make it through during a 'rage' where wind and tide are against each other – how some of the cuts are easier than others. We consulted our trusty *Explorer Chartbook* of the Exumas, where detailed descriptions of all of the cuts up and down the Exumas chain are available. Big Rock Cut, which is the body of water that separates Little Majors Spot from Staniel Cay providing access to Exuma Sound, was right there handy for us. We had been scoping it out for a few days, and it looked pretty benign. A reconnaissance trip, out through the cut in our dinghy with our handheld depth sounder, confirmed that it was wide enough, deep enough, and appeared to be very doable. Even though it was not rated as the best of cuts, we figured that with the right timing, it shouldn't present any obvious problems. The decision was made – we were heading off to the outside.

OFF TO GEORGE TOWN – We decided to head out at dawn. Since we were going to be in the deep water of Exuma Sound for this trip, we didn't need to concern ourselves with the usual late departure to allow for a high sun and the associated visibility. We motored uneventfully through Big Rock Cut just after daybreak. Contingency plans allowed for stopping at Farmers Cay, entering at either Farmers Cut or Galliot Cut. As it turned out we had an uneventful passage, trolling from the cockpit along the way with a rigged ballyhoo that we had bought at the Staniel Cay marina. The fishing was unsuccessful but the trip was a significant accomplishment. In our rush to 'catch up' with our imagined schedule, we had successfully managed to *not* see a large portion of the Exuma Cays, a high point of the trip for many Bahamas cruisers. Not all of the rush was manufactured. We had been in contact on the single side band with our friends Bonnie and Roger on the catamaran *Kokomo* who had just arrived in George Town. They had been on a cruise down in the Jumentos and had just returned to George Town for a few days for provisioning before heading off to the eastern Bahamas for more cruising. We pulled in at Conch Cay Cut at the north end of George Town's Elizabeth Harbour and dropped the hook in the Kidd's Cove anchorage at about 4:30 in the afternoon. Not a bad day. We had managed to fish and make water for over six hours during the trip.

We visited Bonnic and Roger, probably our very best sailing friends, whom we had not seen since we all left Baltimore harbor the previous summer. We had been dockside liveaboard neighbors for three years there. They took us on a tour of the George Town scene – shopping at the *Exuma Market*, internet service access at a nearby provider, a stop at the *Scotia Bank* ATM, lunch at the *Peace 'n' Plenty*, a walk around Lake Victoria. It was great to see them, but next day they were off to the east for some more Bahama cruiser events.

One day while we were anchored, there was a meeting on the beach announced on the VHF radio. It was to be held out on volleyball beach and any interested 'southbound cruisers' were invited to attend. Now neither of us is very much attracted to group events, but out of curiosity we checked it out. We attended and, more or less as expected, we found a group of what appeared to be the blind leading the blind. Rumors were rampant, how-to information from those who had never done the trip, and advice of all sorts from people who just like to participate in group events (and George Town is awash in those people all season long) was offered. There even seemed to be a small cult of Bruce Van Sant worshipers who were there to dispute any advice that seemed the least bit contrary to his book. When one cruiser got up and started addressing the subject of how he intended to carry his guns down through the islands, an obviously inalienable right of all American cruisers and an essential aspect of cruising the islands, we felt it was time to leave. The entire affair proved to be more unsettling than helpful. All in all not a particularly productive learning experience.

One unanticipated positive thing that did come out of our George Town stay was our obtaining a copy of the CYC charts for the Caribbean. We had redundant sets of charts on disk covering the entire Caribbean, but we never like to be without paper charts. Since we had some paper charts of some of the South American coast but not for the Caribbean, we arranged a trade with another cruising boat in the harbor. One of the businesses in George Town had a Xerox-type blueprint copier where cruisers were welcome to go and, for a very reasonable fee, make copies of charts. The resulting copies were in black and white, were not waterproof, and were not on the greatest quality paper, but they would function in a pinch – exactly what we wanted. In exchange for his copying our charts that he lacked, he allowed us to copy his entire set of CYC charts, which we lacked. Everybody came out ahead, and at a very modest cost.

A day or so after our arrival, we did a dinghy tour of Elizabeth Harbour, checking out the south entrance where we anticipated staging out for our departure in a few days. Once we had finished our provisioning, socialized with our friends, attended any useless meetings that were available, and dispensed with a variety of miscellaneous tasks, we were prepared to leave. what appeared to be an excellent weather window was approaching, Bruce Van Sant's book had described staging out to the southern anchorage, which would allow a faster exit from Elizabeth Harbour. In spite of the fact that most cruisers tend to measure their stay at George Town in weeks, we were ready to leave after just four days. With the approach of what appeared to be an ideal weather opportunity, we set out for the Red Shank channel and our staging point near Fowl Cay.

Now, we didn't see it at the time because we were wrapped up in it, but in retrospect it seems that by this time we had developed something of an obsession over weather windows. At this point we were beginning to get good at differentiating a really good weather opportunity from one that was just going to be so-so. Granted, we were eager to get to the Dominican Republic. It was one of our objectives on this trip to spend a substantial time in the DR, enjoying the people, the culture, the history, and spending some time working on our Spanish. However we were still mostly concerned about our late start and the possibility that at some point one of these weather windows might just be our last opportunity to make our necessary easting. We realize now that we should have taken our time coming down through the Exumas. We should have stopped in George Town and actually enjoyed some of the activities and the variety of people encountered there. We should have lived and enjoyed a little of the 'snowbird' lifestyle. But at the time we had other things on our minds. We were on a mission.

CONCERNS ABOUT WEATHER – It was along about this time that we had a discussion with Chris Parker one morning on the HF radio during his weather net. We were concerned about our upcoming passage from the Turks and Caicos to the Dominican Republic. Having heard some mention of the problems of making this relatively short but potentially treacherous crossing and the need for a proper weather front in order to moderate conditions sufficiently to allow a comfortable crossing, we were wondering just how much longer those fronts would continue to play a role. After all, it was March and Spring was approaching. How much longer would those fronts continue to produce the necessary effect we needed to allow us to make the trip? Each day as we avidly listened to his weather report and discussions, we had heard the calls from boats that were down in the Turks and Caicos and on this particular day we addressed our concerns with Chris.

In his response he stated that the fronts that regularly swept through the area would continue until probably about late April, at which time they start to weaken in strength and diminish in their frequency. He described the effect that the fronts have on moderating the wind and seas as they drop down from the north and west, decreasing the strength of the trade winds and/or causing them to shift in direction, often allowing a more comfortable sail to the south by slightly easterly direction required to get from the southern Turks and Caicos down to Luperón in the Dominican Republic.

Unfortunately we had a minor communication problem. He

was thinking that we were looking for hardy and boisterous but comfortable *sail* across this stretch of water, while we were only concerned with making a *comfortable* passage. Sailing is nice but *sailing* was nowhere near *comfortable* on our list of priorities. Evidently we didn't make this clear in our inquiry. So we continued along our merry way under the misconception that if we didn't make our DR crossing by late April, then it was likely that, in the absence of those moderating cold fronts, we would probably have a much less comfortable trip across.

The unspoken facts of the situation became much more evident to us once we arrived in Luperón and were sitting at anchor watching others arrive. The longer we sat there, the milder the crossings became for those boats that came in later in the season. Chris was right when he told us that the later in the season and the closer to summer it gets, the fewer and further between and the weaker the passing cold fronts become. What went unsaid in our conversation, mainly because we just didn't ask the right question, was that the weather in general moderates in the southern Atlantic and the Caribbean as summer draws nearer. The *cold fronts become unnecessary for making the crossing* because the trade winds become weaker, the lulls in the trades grow more frequent all on their own, and the seas moderate *significantly*. Chris was right. With the approach of summer, it becomes more and more difficult to get decent *sailing* conditions. However, if you just want an easy and pleasant motorsail across that stretch, conditions start to optimize in May and June and those conditions (if you ignore the increasing tropical storm threat) continue throughout the summer months! Similar consideration could be applied toward crossing the Mona Passage and the Anegada (Sombrero) Passage. As it turns out, we could easily have spent an additional two months exploring and enjoying the Bahamas and the Turks and Caicos and still have made it to the DR with plenty of time to hunker down safely in advance of hurricane season. Isn't hindsight a wonderful thing!

Obviously, if you were anticipating only a brief stop in the DR and then traveling on down to spend storm season in Grenada or Venezuela, you would prefer to make your crossing to the DR earlier – perhaps late April or early May. On the other hand, if you are not bound by insurance company dictates and you intend to hide out in the DR for hurricane season, it would not be unreasonable to just linger in the Turks and Caicos indefinitely, while keeping a very close watch on the weather. At the first hint of any sort of system developing, the safety and security of the DR's north coast is only hours away. Just don't get taken by surprise.

RUM CAY - OR NOT – Rum Cay was to be the beginning of our exploration of the southeast Bahamas. We realized we had missed most of the Exumas, but we felt that it was too late to change that. However, the reefs and the snorkeling opportunities present in the southeast Bahamas are renowned. Rum Cay, San Salvador, Conception, Mayaguana – much of the best the Bahamas has to offer presents itself in these out-islands. In addition, for the southbound cruiser the longer distances required to visit the islands of the far Bahamas start to test your resolve and your weather interpretation talents. It was here that we learned to look for longer windows – weather opportunities where there was an element of padding, a built-in extra day or two on each end of a necessary window, so there would be no surprises from an unexpected premature change in the weather during a passage. In the Exumas serviceable anchorages were a short couple of hours or less apart. In the southern islands, a passage required most of a day to get to an anchorage that might or might not give us protection that we felt was appropriate for any impending weather.

After spending a quiet night at anchor in the waters to the south of Fowl Cay, at daybreak we weighed anchor and headed east via the Three-Fathom Channel and turning north into the relatively deep cut of Whelk Harbour. We headed out of Elizabeth Harbour on a northwesterly course with Fowl Cay to our west and Whelk Cay to our east. Our weather forecast sounded too good to be true. We headed up over the top of Cape Santa Maria on Long Island with just a light breeze, forecast to turn to light and variable, ideal for motorsailing upwind and making the best time under the most comfortable conditions.

Once we had rounded Cape Santa Maria and were headed for Rum Cay we just couldn't resist the urge to keep going. We looked at each other and decided Mayaguana was within an easy overnight trip. Change of plans. All systems go for Mayaguana.

Plans of snorkeling and enjoying the beautiful, pristine waters of Flamingo Bay or Port Nelson on Rum Cay instantly morphed into plans for exploring the reefs and turquoise water of Abrahams Bay. We always told everybody, as do most cruisers, that our plans from day to day and week to week were chiseled in mud. And so it goes.

Late in the night, as we were motoring along making excellent time, things began to change. The breeze seemed to fill in a little from the east and the seas started to build just ever so slightly. By daybreak we were pounding into some sizable headseas. Here we were, being presented with one of those above-mentioned surprises from an unexpected premature change in the weather. (Ahoy! Learning experience!) We flirted with the idea of stopping in the less sheltered waters of Plana Cay to wait out this unexpected change in the weather. Before committing to any course of action, we waited for Chris Parker's 6 AM Caribbean weather on the SSB and the news was not what we wanted to hear. Winds were now predicted to pick up from the east and would continue to remain in that quadrant for the next few days. We were still over thirty miles from our planned stop in Mayaguana.

Change of plans. Annie grabbed the chartbook for the Far Bahamas and started searching. About 10 miles behind us was a large bay with what looked like outstanding protection. A quick turnaround and suddenly the weather improved remarkably. Our miserable slog to windward was instantly transformed into a pleasant downwind sail with just hint of waddle as we enjoyed a relaxing motorsail back toward Acklins Island and the anticipated shelter of Atwood Harbour. On paper our prospective anchorage looked excellent and, according to the *Explorer*

Chartbook we could expect nothing in the way of facilities – virtually complete isolation.

ATWOOD HARBOUR, ACKLINS ISLAND – We approached the entrance to Atwood Harbour using our electronic charts to locate the cut through the surrounding reef. Typical of the islands in the southwest Bahamas, an extensive but mostly submerged barrier reef system runs along the outer, exposed coast of Acklins Island and its associated smaller cays, extending up and around to encircle nearby Crooked Island. This wall is interrupted periodically by a small cut which, with local knowledge and/or a combination of good charts and a sharp eye, will allow the careful navigator to get through. As we neared the cut, with the breeze eased by the proximity of the nearby shoreline and with one of us on the bow to serve as lookout, we carefully motored through the opening and into the sheltering arms of a spacious tropical bay.

We had crossed the Tropic of Cancer at some time during the night so we were now officially in the tropics – and suddenly, with the island breaking the breeze and our anchor splashing the surface of the tourmaline water, it really felt tropical. It was mid-morning as we dropped the hook and watched our *Delta* settle into the sandy bottom and we sat back to take in our surroundings. We were the lone vessel in an anchorage that in a more populated area might have been crowded with fifty or even a hundred boats. Nestled into the northwest shoreline of Lady Slipper Cay and with the northeastern point of Acklins providing protection to the west, this bay provides nearly 300 degrees of protection, extending from nearly the north-northeast around to the east and south all the way around almost to the northwest. The bay is considered to be an excellent refuge so long as the wind blows from any direction except northerly. Under those circumstances, it is definitely *not* a good place to get caught.

After our twenty-four hour passage we enjoyed an early morning dinner of salmon and yellow rice and flopped out to catch some z's. Later in the day another, apparently northbound, sailboat hove into view flying a DR courtesy flag and anchored a hundred meters or so off our stern just to spend the night.

The following day we dumped five jerry jugs of fuel into our tanks. This left us in need Consulting our reference sources we determined that fuel availability at our next stop, Mayaguana, was limited. It would require a stop in the bay at Northwest Point. This no doubt would have been a very interesting stop for us, but not having any familiarity with the island, the northern exposure of the bay made us a little uncomfortable. With the continuous parade of fronts coming through, our experience (limited though it was) suggested that we would probably be much less likely to get caught by surprise if we kept to the waters of Abrahams Bay which would keep the island mass to the north of us.

Under our given circumstances, the wisdom of that decision happened to be borne out by our proper choice of weather windows. However, in retrospect now with the perfect vision of hindsight, I can vouch for just how treacherous Abrahams Bay can become if you happen to be there when the wind swings around to the east or south. On our return trip from the Caribbean, we elected to make an emergency stop in Abrahams Bay to escape an unexpected weather system. Thinking that we would tuck in there on the spur of the moment to rest for the night, coming in after dark we were unable to get far enough into the bay to get any relief from wind and seas. As a result we spent an anxious and miserable night of fitful, if any, sleep bucking against our anchor. It was such a miserable situation that at first light we elected to yank our anchor, only with some difficulty since we use a manual windlass, and make a run for it, heading downwind toward the Exumas. We felt fortunate just to escape unscathed.

Back to the issue at hand, we decided we needed to fill up our jugs. We never like to leave ourselves at the mercy of the unknown when we can avoid it. Since we weren't going to refuel at Mayaguana, that meant that our next fuel op would not be until the Turks and Caicos. The *Explorer Chartbook* made mention that fuel on Acklins Island was a long way from Atwood Harbour. Being isolated in a bay with apparently no one anywhere nearby, we decided to get on the VHF and see what we might find. Within just moments we received a response, loud and clear, from a Captain Bradley, skipper of the *Lady Barbara*, a local fishing charter. He suggested we load up our jugs and take our dinghy around the western point of our bay and into nearby Lovely Bay where he would meet us. His directions for following the channel through the reef sounded pretty straightforward, just "follow the green water about 50 to 100 feet inside the breaker line," to get through to lovely bay. The trip was about four or five miles by dinghy.

After an hour of winding our way in and out through the maze of reefs that all seemed just barely awash, we ended up in the wide open spaces of Lovely Bay. The forty foot fishing charter *Lady Barbara* was anchored not far off shore. We made a deal with Captain Bradley to drive us to the nearest fuel depot in his Mitsubishi Minivan. During the drive of twenty or more miles to Spring Point and the fuel station, a large rack of fuel drums stored on racks behind a house (just across the street from what appeared to be a very modern multiple island gas station which was under construction and nearing completion), we were updated on some of the regional history and current events by Captain Bradley, bar/restaurant owner and local mayor from the nearby settlement of Chesters and former member of the Bahamian legislature. Mission accomplished, on the way back we stopped at McKinney's Store and bought a few items. In order to avoid the extra weight and draft as we worked our way back through the reefs from Lovely Bay, we dropped our five full fuel jugs off on the beach above Atwood Harbour before we ended up back at the *Lady Barbara*'s anchorage.

Captain Bradley's statement that he routinely took the forty-plus foot *Lady Barbara* back and forth between Atwood Harbour and Lovely Bay following his described route through the reef only served to make us feel even more self-conscious on our return trip about our inability to get through without playing the part of a ball knocking from bumper to bumper inside a pinball machine. In any event, we eventually managed to get back to Atwood, retrieve our jugs from the beach, and return to *Fidelis* before dusk, the better part of a full day of travel and another successful adventure behind us. All in all we were impressed with the cooperative nature and cordial attitude of everybody we met that day. The people of Acklins Island certainly made a most memorable impression on both of us.

We spent the next day, Easter Sunday, aboard, as we prepared things for the next leg of our journey. Another sailboat, *Pennywhistle*, had come into the bay to replace our other earlier departed neighbor, and had anchored a hundred yards off our bow, near the eastern shoreline. As we kicked back and *Fidelis* gently tugged at her chain, we contemplated the next leg of our trip while indulging our exploratory urges in some serious beachcombing. We enjoyed Easter dinner in the seclusion of our island paradise. Next day we got word from Chris Parker's Caribbean weather net that winds were about to come around to the southwest the following day, which should allow us to finally escape from our weather-enforced rest and continue on to Mayaguana.

In the morning, with the wind clocked around to the southwest, we retrieved our anchor and headed out through the mouth of the bay and the outlying cut. Not long after leaving the harbor, we saw our new neighbor *Pennywhistle* also working their way out and following in our wake. The day was developing into a beauty and our conditions were ideal for the trip. We raised Mayaguana on the eastern horizon by midafternoon and were dropping anchor in Abrahams Bay at 5:00 PM. We had reached the bottom of the Bahamas and our weather window looked good for still another leg.

MAYAGUANA – We dropped the hook in the late afternoon in about thirteen feet of water, a quarter mile or so inside the entrance to Abrahams Bay. As expected, the bay was absolutely humongous and, according to our charts with the number of coral heads increasing dramatically as you travel closer to shore, a dinghy trip to shore to explore was not very realistic from this far out. Plus, we were enjoying only the very beginning of what appeared to be a very generous weather window. We figured this window would be better spent crossing to the Turks and Caicos where we could get in some provisioning, refuel, and maybc spend a little time exploring.

Once again we had a little bit of that sensation of being at anchor out in the middle of the ocean, with the shoreline nearly a mile off to the northwest and extending several miles off to the northeast. As we sat in our cockpit the surface of the water was flat calm and the open, unbroken expanse extending from the east around to the south and west gave no hint of the treacherous reef that all but encircles this bay. We discussed how easily it would be for someone with no charts and no local knowledge to end up on the reef without any forewarning whatsoever.

Several other boats were anchored, some northbound, returning from a wintertime stay in the Caribbean, others like us, on their way south, ready to leave the Bahamas behind and embark on a new adventure. Our grand plan had been to stage out to Southeast Point as advised in the *Gentleman's Guide* for our exit to Provo, but our weather forecast was such that we felt such a move wasn't really unnecessary. If we left at first light the next morning, we would have a good long day to get to the Caicos Bank directly from Abrahams Bay, and we should still have adequate daylight to visually navigate our way into the anchorage at Sapodilla Bay. Since our weather was holding just fine, if we ran out of light on the banks we could just drop the hook and continue the following day.

We left in the morning and headed out. Once we got through the mouth of the bay, we steered a southeasterly course, following the course shown in our *Explorer Chartbook*, toward the sandbore channel entrance at the western edge of the Caicos Bank. We still had one slightly used, rigged ballyhoo in the refrigerator, left over from our stop back in Staniel Cay, so we dropped him over the side for a little trolling. In the early afternoon, as we were approaching the banks, we saw something dragging in the water far behind the boat. We pulled in our line along with a beautiful mahi-mahi. About thirty inches long, he weighed in at about six pounds – a little small for a mahi, but still a tasty supper and at least one more meal for the two of us.

We crossed onto the Caicos Bank shortly after three in the afternoon and dropped anchor in Sapodilla Bay about two hours later, just a little too late for check-in. After some routine engine maintenance we sat and relished the results of a totally uneventful crossing, sipping our sundowners as we prepared our mahi steaks.

Patch reefs on the Caicos Bank.

The Customs House in Alice Town, Bimini. Bahamian government buildings are painted a distinctive coral pink color.

What About the Bahamas?

♦ Pros
  - Zillions of islands
    - One of the world's largest cruising grounds
  - The gold standard of tropical cruising
    - Most cruisers are familiar with Bahamas cruising and will compare cruising there with cruising elsewhere
    - Cruisers from Europe, Australia, Africa can be heard comparing Red Sea, South Pacific, Indian Ocean cruising to the Bahamas
    - Remember, cruisers are there during the worst time of the year
      - Most favorable conditions are in the summer but you can't be there then
    - FYI - The Bahamas are NOT in the Caribbean
      - Cruise ship lines and airlines often advertise the Bahamas as being 'the most beautiful islands in the Caribbean'
      - Not that the Caribbean is that big a deal, just need to keep our geography straight

♦ Cons
  - Limited storm protection
    - The islands are low and offer little protection
  - Bahamas are a common hurricane target
  - Constant parade of fronts during the winter
  - Water is cold in the wintertime
    - My principal complaint
  - People are unfriendly (?)
    - We have heard this from a number of cruisers but do not feel that it is true.
    - Americans have a tendency to expect that 'artificial friendliness' that we encounter on a regular basis at businesses and from businesspeople in the U.S. on a daily basis
      - Bahamians tend to be much more genuine
        - Just try a genuine 'Good morning' or 'Good day' and see the response you get

Providenciales, or 'Provo,' largest of the Caicos Islands

Next day, the last day of March, David dinghied in to the south dock for the check-in, a reasonable US $5.00 at the time. Since the shoal waters of the Turks and Caicos banks were not all that attractive to us with our nearly seven foot draft, the idea of an extended visit was not particularly appealing to us. For those interested in staying longer than a week for some exploration, a cruising permit was only about US $50.00.

Our first full day there, Annie walked into "town," a bit of a stretch for the word when describing what Providenciales has to offer, and after a record amount of walking picked up a ride back to the anchorage. In the meantime, some exploring by dinghy revealed that fuel was not readily available anywhere near the Sapodilla Bay anchorage. In addition, unfortunately garbage disposal was no more readily available than was fuel. The lack of garbage facilities, combined with the frequently lazy or inconsiderate nature of many cruisers and native islanders was more than obvious with just a short walk along the bay.

Over the next two days we did some provisioning, not the most convenient procedure from our anchorage. After hitchhiking into town and renting a small Daihatsu from the local *Budget Car Rental* we spent the a day filling fuel jugs, visiting various grocery stores, the local *NAPA* auto store, an ATM machine for cash, and having a rather heated dispute with the providers of our *MasterCard* who were somewhat overzealously looking out for our financial interests. The next day, on our way to return the car we stopped at Turks & Caicos Gas to fill one of our propane tanks, which had run out while we were in Atwood Harbour, and we also stopped in at the local marine store to look for a couple of things.

A fresh weather window was about to present itself and we were done with Provo, finished with our errands and provisioning. It was time for us to head down and across the Caicos Bank, then across the Turks Passage to the protection of Sand Cay, our launching point for the crossing to Luperón and the Dominican Republic.

The following morning, a Sunday, dawned clear. No Chris

Parker weather report on Sunday, but Saturday's forecast had called for a long, favorable weather window. We left at first light, ready to "Bruce" our way through this next leg of the thorny path. In his *Gentleman's Guide*, there was a comment to the effect that over the years Bruce had made this trip many times in his old *Formosa* ketch, *Jalan Jalan*, with her 6 ½ foot draft and he described his route southward from Sapodilla Bay to the central bank area. He made mention that, by following this route he could leave early, before the sun was high enough for good visibility, because he knew there was plenty of water for passage of a 6 ½ foot draft. We made the mistake of interpreting that description just a tad too literally. As the first couple of dark patches passed, we posted a lookout on the bow, only to see a dark area in the water dead ahead. Our reaction was a little slow as we passed over the top of the patch. The ensuing crunch was the sound of lightweight staghorn coral meeting the fiberglass-encased concrete and lead keel of a CSY, not really a fair matchup. We felt bad to have damaged some of nature's handiwork, but also very fortunate that it was staghorn and not a stand of elkhorn or brain coral – bottom line, no detectable damage to the hull, not to mention we learned a long-remembered lesson.

The sunlight filled in on this beautiful, clear day in April and our bow lookout was able to stand down as the patches of coral began to show up well in the distance. After several miles heading to the southeast, we swung around to an easterly course and headed across the bank toward Sand Cay. Dark patches of coral, ranging in size from small to an acre or more, were visible all the way across the bank. Most of the time when we passed close abeam of one of these patches, it appeared to be mostly the same sort of lightweight staghorn coral. On occasion, however, some of the reefs appeared to be much thicker and heavier in appearance, not to mention much closer to the surface.

We began to lose our light in the mid-afternoon, again requiring posting of a bow watch. At about four o'clock we headed off the banks into the deeper water of the Turks Island

Passage and aimed our bow toward Sand Cay. We dropped anchor just after complete darkness in about fourteen feet of water in the lee of Sand Cay, an island that seemed so steep-to that, coming in in the dark under GPS alone, we might actually have run into it if we had not been exercising caution. Since there was no moon we stopped, shut down the engine, and stood on deck and listened for the surf on the beach before restarting and proceeding until we felt we were close enough without being in too close. As we flipped on the anchor light and turned in, we discussed catching Monday morning's weather report to confirm what we had heard on Saturday with the intention of leaving for Luperón, but regardless, the plan was to stay there for as long as necessary before heading south.

Next day when we came on deck we found the bottom was clear and sandy with good holding. We were sitting in the lee of a small island with a sandy knoll and an obviously non-working light, evident from our dark approach the night previous, on top. We turned on the SSB radio to catch Chris Parker's weather and waited but no report was forthcoming. An inquiry on the radio garnered a surprising response. Evidently we had missed the part of Chris's report on Saturday wherein he had announced that his antenna would be down and under construction on Sunday and Monday, and that he would therefore not be on doing a report again until Tuesday – not at all the news we wanted to hear.

We already had a report from Chris that our weather window was in good shape for a DR crossing and was projected to last for several days, however that weather forecast was now two days old. In accordance with our now well-developed habits (which we in turn had acquired from the reading of Bruce's book), we were not comfortable with making this move based on a two day old report, yet we were reluctant to sit and wait several more days should we find out the next day that the window was now going to close prematurely.

As we were discussing Chris Parker's non-appearance on the radio, *Yellow Rose*, a boat we had never met before who was apparently was quite nearby, broke in on the SSB with their own quite favorable and very current weather report. We inquired where their report had come from and were informed that they had gotten it from another boat who had taken it from a satellite source. In any event, the report was very positive, calling for light breezes from the east, mild seas, and no expected change over the ensuing few days. They declared that they were thinking of going for it, and asked if we were. *Yellow Rose* seemed to have confidence in their report and the source, and we considered. We looked at one another. This was exactly the reenforcement that we needed in order to make our decision. Again however, it was totally contrary to the principals espoused in the *Gentleman's Guide* (and again, in our experience, with good reason).

We reviewed our weather scenario: a great weather window projecting out for several days but from a forecast that was now two days old; a confirming report from a second, but, to us at the time, very questionable source; and, finally, no visible suggestion of impending change in the weather evident in the sky, the breeze, or the seas. In the words of Bob Dylan, "the line it is drawn, the curse it is cast." We locked ourselves in and decided to call it a "go." We called back *Yellow Rose* and informed them as to our decision. They were departing shortly from Cockburn Town on South Caicos Island and would be passing by us sometime in mid to late afternoon. We didn't know it yet, but we were to eventually become friends and spend some time with Gary and Renatta, the Texans aboard *Yellow Rose*.

At this point we were surprised by a "break" in our radio conversation by two other boats who had obviously been listening in. Obviously they were interested in the weather, but they seemed to be *more* interested in crossing with a fleet. They wanted to know if, since we were going, could they cross over with us? Can you actually say "no" to somebody who asks that sort of question? Last thing I knew any boat is free to cross any body of water at pretty much any time (except Americans headed for Cuba under George W., of course) regardless of who else happens to have the same plans. Here we were with the fleet forming up sometime in midafternoon. After violating some of our (and Bruce's) most basic tenets, we lay down for a little rest before heading out for this overnighter. At this point we were no longer "Brucin' it" as I had come to call our upwind venture; we were now flying by the seat of our pants.

Annie's Dark Chocolate Rum Cake Recipe
(Don't tell *anybody*. It's a secret.)

1 Dark chocolate cake mix
4 eggs
1 cup sour cream
1 packet instant chocolate pudding
1 cup semi-sweet chocolate chips
1 Tbsp vanilla
4 Tbsp Rum
½ cup vegetable oil

Mix all ingredients at medium speed for ten minutes.
Pour into a greased Bundt pan.
Bake at 350°F for 55 minutes.
Cool for 15 minutes before removing from pan.

Big Sand Cay

So, What About the Turks & Caicos?

♦ Pros
    - Geophysically you are still in the Bahamas
        - From 1965 until Bahamian independence in 1973 they were politically part of the Bahamas
    - Caicos and Turks Banks are simply smaller versions of the Bahamas Banks
    - Same positive attributes as the Bahamas

♦ Cons
    - Little protection offered except for very shoal draft vessels
    - Still get the same pesky fronts
    - Still get those pesky hurricanes

Making music at a bar in Luperón

We pulled our anchor around three in the afternoon. Our weather information called for breezes in the ten to twelve knot range, reportedly to be accompanied by small seas. In hopes of a reasonably enjoyable sail most of the way across to the DR, we had chosen to leave a couple of hours earlier than we otherwise would have for a motoring trip. We headed south out the mouth of the Turks Passage, making certain to give Endymion Rock a well-deserved margin of safety, before leaning a bit to the east of our course to allow for our projected leeway over the next fifteen to eighteen hours. After all, in spite of projected light winds and a mild seaway, a significant east to west current tends to rip through this river of water that races on its westerly course between the high ground of the Bahamas/Turks/Caicos Banks to the north and the massive islands of the Greater Antilles to the south.

As the nighttime approached, our light breeze started to die out and turned into more of a light and variable. *Fidelis* is a big old boat and it takes a fair breeze to keep her moving. The seas were small, but they were dead on the beam and our sails just wouldn't stay full. We fired up the engine and started motoring under just the main. Kicking it up to over four knots kept the main full which provided a tremendous improvement in the quality of our ride. The only problem with motoring was that we were likely to make landfall a little too early in the morning.

During the night we spotted a couple of ships off in the distance, but for the most part things were uneventful. It was not until a while after we had reached the halfway point in our crossing that we noticed the approach of a huge black cloud, blotting out everything in its path and rolling toward us from the south. Gary on *Yellow Rose*, who had a radar unit, had earlier called to warn us of an approaching squall. In anticipation of the worst, we had already shortened sail, battened down, and prepared ourselves and the boat for what might possibly be a major wind squall. As it came toward us we could see no lightning, and when it eventually arrived there was no lightning or thunder. But as the darkness of the cloud seemed to swallow us, there was a sudden shifting gust of wind which quickly died off to nothing and left us at the mercy of the short rolls of the small seas. It was a little spooky and a bit uncomfortable, but it amounted to no threat, and we could see another large black cloud not far off, again rolling down on us. *Yellow Rose* continued to periodically call on the VHF to advise of additional oncoming squall clouds or to point out a yet to be visualized ship in the distance. The big dark cloud scenario repeated itself periodically until morning, sometimes a gust of wind, sometimes some spitting of light rain, most of the time just a complete dying off of what little breeze we had.

As the weak greyness of dawn approached we began to see the high, undulating contours of Hispaniola begin to take shape from the mass of black in front of us. We slowed down and stood off for a bit to wait for better daylight. A short time later, with *Yellow Rose*, a black-hulled *Krogen* 38, out in the lead, we approached our waypoint for the mouth of the bay and called in to Luperón harbor in hopes that someone might hear and come out to lead us in. Most of the markers appeared to be present and on station, but the channel in close to the harbor entrance is a little touchy, especially for a deeper draft vessel. One of the cruisers in the harbor came out to lead us in, a gesture that was greatly appreciated. We found a spot in 18 feet of water and dropped the hook a little before 9 AM with the rest of our flotilla, *Wounded Spirit* and *JJ*, arriving less than an hour behind us.

It wasn't long before the officials started to show up, some such as the agricultural officials charging official fees for which we received government receipts, others such as the comandante's office (the navy) and the customs officials requested 'fees' and 'donations' that may have been a little more questionable. Once the on-board check-in festivities were finished, it was time to dinghy into town and visit the immigration and the port authority offices, located just up the street from the *muelle* (the docks). At that time, April of 2005, it cost us just under US $100 to complete all of our entrance formalities. In addition, upon departure there was a US $15 per month 'harbor fee' for our time spent anchored in the harbor, which was due before we could receive our clearance. These fees have very likely changed since that time.

The Dominican peso usually hovers somewhere around 30 to 35:1 with the US dollar. When we were there it ranged from about 28 to 32 or so, depending upon whether you were buying or selling.

A few things to keep in mind about staying in Luperón: 1) There are some moorings in the harbor. Don't use them, and especially don't *pay* anybody to use them. Sometimes under just modest trade wind conditions boats tied to them will start sailing around the harbor like they're off to a regatta. We don't know what they're tied to – heard rumors of old car engines, old anchors, or whatever. 2) The anchor of choice in the mangrove mud of Luperón harbor is more or less universally agreed upon to be the *Bruce*, but also large *Danforth/Fortress* types work well too. It is generally acknowledged that plows, including the *CQR*, do NOT hold very well there. There are various hypotheses that have been advanced regarding this. Obviously if you have a plow that is significantly oversized relative to your boat size, it is much more likely to hold. 3) When anchoring there, it is recommended that you use about a 10:1 or better scope for the first few days until your hook has buried itself well into the substrate, at which point you can shorten your scope down to as little as 4 or 5:1 and hold well under virtually any wind and sea conditions. We preferred to keep it at no less than 5 or 6:1. 4) The tide causes boats at anchor to circle their anchors usually at least once a day. It took us two years to get the kinks out of our anchor chain after spending eight months in Luperón, and that was in spite of the fact that we turned our boat in a circle a few times, a couple of times each week while we were there, using our dinghy, in an attempt to unwind it. 5) Be aware that the harbor is extremely nutrient rich and most people find it very unattractive to get in the water. You should expect to clean your boat's bottom (or have it cleaned) on average about once every three to six weeks because of the extreme rate of bottom growth.

Leaving Luperón harbor

On the approach to Luperón we used the instructions in Bruce Van Sant's book to help with the entrance to the outer harbor, at which point we made our radio request for somebody to guide us in. We navigated around the harbor and found a spot with room for us to drop the hook.

You also may be asked by someone, usually the military representative, either upon your arrival or upon departure (or both), for a 'donation' or 'tip.' It's your choice whether or not you pay it. Last time I (David) passed through, I was in the harbor only overnight and elected not to pay it, with no repercussions.

When we arrived in the Dominican Republic we took on the challenge of learning to use their *gua-guas*, a means of transportation that falls between the cheaper but much more risky *motoconcho* (a motorbike taxi service, where a person [or even two people] just gets on behind the driver and rides to their

Motoconcho corner in downtown Luperón, DR

WARNING! About half of the cruisers who stop in Luperón decide to rent one of the inexpensive motorbikes available there. About half of those who do, get injured – some quite seriously.

---

chosen destination – talk about putting your life in the hands of a total stranger!) and the much more expensive local taxis. Every town has its *motoconcho* corner, its *gua-gua* stop, and its taxi stand. The taxi drivers were a little resentful that some of us 'rich gringos' chose to ride with the locals in the *gua-guas* for $2 or $3 each instead of paying their $40 or $50 for a trip to Puerto Plata. But many of the cruisers found *gua-gua* travel to be unthinkable (rub shoulders with the locals? – you must be kidding!). Always ask the driver the price in advance – and also, if you can, quietly ask one of the local passengers to make sure you are paying what they are paying.

Driving yourself in the DR is, to put it mildly, an adventure. A couple of other cruising couples in the harbor bought cars for their stay (a huge mistake – the locals definitely see you coming) and drove regularly (or as regularly as they could in the pathetic vehicles that they had bought). We chose to pass on this particular experience.

If you have not been to the DR, a *gua-gua* is a compact car (Toyota Corolla or similar type) or a tiny microvan (Mitsubishi or similar) and they have fixed routes, like buses in the U.S. They line up at the *gua-gua* stop and will generally have some type of sign to let you know where they go. You get in and wait until the car is full or the driver feels that he has enough passengers to make it worthwhile to go, then he leaves. Along the route he will drop off or pick up passengers. They will stop when the *gua-gua* gets to the end of its prescribed route, or you can ask the driver to stop wherever you want to get out along the route.

It seldom matters whether or not the car or van is full, people just keep getting in. Our record number of people that we rode with in one of the small vans was twenty-seven including the driver. Even the locals were amused and counting on that one. For a small car, one day we had six people in the front and six people in the back at one point – the driver had the door open and a lady sitting on his lap for about a mile or two of the trip before someone finally got out and allowed things to return to some semblance of normal. At one time I (David) was riding in the back seat of an automobile type *gua-gua* and felt some mild sharp pokes in my right ankle. When we got further down the road the man sitting next to me got out. As he left he reached down on the floor beside me and scooped up a chicken!

By the way, please don't get carried away with your tipping. You're not impressing anybody and it's the hot-shot big tipper throwing his money at the 'poor islanders' that makes things miserable for those of us who tip reasonably. Most of those Dominicans who deal with the tourists do relatively well compared to the general populace. When somebody gives a tip that is equal to the normal cost of a given service, it doesn't take long before they just see all of us as suckers, eager to be parted from our dollars.

A few words of warning are in order about the local motorbike rentals. We know more people who have been hurt riding motorbikes in the DR, and more who have been seriously injured doing it, than all of the boating-related accidents we have heard about in our fifteen years of sailing.

Road hazards in the DR are widespread.

Small motorcycles are ubiquitous in the DR. We have seen motorbikes transporting objects as large as a 100 pound propane tank or a full-sized washing machine, and we have seen entire families of four or five

147

people riding on one bike.

They are one of the primary modes of transportation for those of less prosperous means in this country and rentals are available at several places in and around Luperón at very reasonable prices. These vehicles are popular among cruisers who find them to be convenient for touring and travel and sometimes rent them for extended tours of the Dominican countryside. However, the often reckless driving style of the Dominicans combined with the sometimes lackadaisical attitude of the visiting cruisers frequently results in accidents and injuries. It is quite common for these ancient easy-rider cruisers who want to relive their Jack Kerouac fantasies to leave the DR with a souvenir "Luperón tattoo" (a case of road rash and/or pipe burns on the legs from dumping their bike) and often much worse. It is challenging to drive a car in the DR, let alone an undersized, underpowered motorbike.

The locals here tend to drive their four-wheeled vehicles with an attitude that is foreign to their gringo counterparts. In a nutshell, the mentality here is that larger vehicles drive as they please and smaller vehicles are expected to give way or simply get run over. Put this on the same road with an American driving style that expects other vehicles to watch out for and yield to smaller vehicles and you have a recipe for disaster. And this doesn't even take into account some of the special characteristics of the Dominican countryside.

A friend of ours while we were there had leased a bike by the month to get the cheaper rate, and he rode it regularly. One day he hit a cow in the road and was seriously hurt. He had to stay in the DR for a number of additional weeks while he recovered from his injuries. Adding insult to injury, he had to pay the owner for the cow since the local DR justice system tends to give tourists the short end of the legal stick.

The most recent serious motorbike accident we have heard about happened to some friends of ours. They were hit by a truck and had the misfortune of spending a couple of days seeing the Dominican public health system from the inside before friends of theirs had them transferred to a private hospital. That was a horror story in itself. They did some serious hospital time and frankly they are both lucky to be alive. Their cruising career may have ended prematurely but fortunately their lives didn't.

These are only a couple of an amazing number of bike injuries sustained. Suppress that urge to take a walk on the wild side. Get those 'born to ride' ya-ya's out of your system someplace else – anywhere else. If you feel you must rent a bike, avoid main highways and high traffic areas and be extremely defensive in your riding style.

A lot of cruisers thought nothing of taking a taxi trip to the city once a week while we were there. And those same cruisers would routinely eat all of their meals at the local yacht club or at one of the local gringo restaurants where the more elaborate meals would commonly cost ten to fifteen U.S. dollars each – not a bad price for the type of meal they ate, but still, that kind of spending adds up in a hurry. When we went out for lunch in the DR we did the local lunch specials where the locals ate, generally about US $3.00 each, and usually had some type of grilled or roasted chicken with beans and rice on the side and we *loved* it. We developed a fondness for beans and rice, fixed in a variety of ways, while we were in the islands that we will never outgrow. All the way down through the islands beans and rice are a staple and you will find them prepared and presented in a variety of ways.

Because of our cooking habits and our repeated need for provisioning trips, it didn't take us long to learn to turn these trips into our own low-cost excursions. In the Dominican Republic there were good grocery stores in Puerto Plata and Santiago, plus there was a *PriceSmart* store in Santiago, which is very similar to a *Sam's Club*. Great place to visit in a chartered taxi with a group of cruisers. Between the local Santiago grocery stores and the *PriceSmart* we could find just about everything (except for brown sugar - really weird in a country that is a major sugar producer). We were only able to find brown sugar (not to be confused with the locally produced sugar, which happens to be kind of brown) at just one market in Puerto Plata.

Another food issue that you should be ready for in the Dominican Republic revolves around the local beef. They produce their own. But it is a far cry from what we were accustomed to eating in the U.S. Although it is abundant, in our opinion (and the opinion of many other North American cruisers) it was just not very good. Even the best steaks have a very rough, gamey flavor that we did not care for. This flavor was even detectable in the burgers that we ate at *McDonald's* and *Burger King*. If you enjoy venison, you probably won't have a problem with the beef. We found the taste objectionable enough that we avoided beef pretty much for our entire stay in the DR.

After several months trapped in Luperón harbor for a record hurricane season we took a few vacations to Santo Domingo, the national capital, down on the Caribbean coast. We would stay at a little hotel we found in Boca Chica, called the *Magic Tropicale*, for US$25 a night, $35 if you wanted air conditioning (which we never do). The hotel was three blocks back from the beach in a neighborhood filled with similar establishments, and they had a beautiful swimming pool and free wireless internet. We would stop in at one of the small local *restaurantes* where the locals eat, and we would eat for next to nothing, or we would buy some food from one of the street vendors and take it back to our room

The *Magic Tropicale* hotel in Boca Chica, east of Santo Domingo, Dominican Republic.

– rather than eating at the local tourist restaurants where the food cost ten times as much. We had a ball there and went several times. The bus ride from downtown Luperón to downtown Santo Domingo cost us about US $5 per person each way, and the subsequent *gua-gua* ride from Santo Domingo to Boca Chica was a couple bucks or so.

You should be aware that the northern coast of the DR is not very cruiser friendly. It is difficult to travel by boat along the coast unless conditions are ideal, which only happens occasionally. Should you venture out and get caught unexpectedly, it may be difficult getting back. The bay at Isabella, several miles west of Luperón, offers some protection under prevailing conditions so long as no northerly swell is running, but the upwind slog to get back to Luperón can be difficult and miserable. To the east of Luperón you can now go to Ocean World near Puerto Plata, but again you must slog your way upwind to do so unless conditions are favorable, and once you have done so it's unlikely you'll want to come back and then have to repeat the trip again when you are ready to leave. Under most circumstances, once you have chosen to leave the harbor you do so with no intention of returning. Therefore the general tendency among cruisers is to hole up for the duration until ready to move on.

> For a number of reasons, geographical, topographical, and meteorological, Luperón harbor is one of the very best hurricane holes in all of the eastern Caribbean region.

If you cruise long enough and you travel as slowly as we did, you may find yourself in some quiet anchorages where you need some imagination to help stave off boredom. Perhaps boredom isn't the correct word to use since it's very hard to imagine being bored while living in paradise. But then, even though we very much enjoyed our stay in Luperón in the Dominican Republic and it was high on our list of places to visit, by most cruiser's standards (ours included) it is not exactly what one would be inclined to describe as 'paradise' either. Anyway, while living on the hook there, I (Annie) found myself looking for activities to keep me amused while Doc was writing his veterinary book.

I (Annie) love to swim, but the waters of Luperón harbor were unanimously considered among cruisers to be less than appealing for a variety of reasons. However I found that I could dinghy from the boat over to the yacht club and walk from there up and over the hill to the local all-inclusive resort, the Luperón Beach Resort. This is where the locals go on holidays and weekends. Although their private amenities such as chairs, tables, and the bars and swimming pools are off-limits to non-registered guests, the general public is welcome to use the beach. The beach here is brushed by the waters of the North Atlantic and the water there is clear, clean, and refreshing. The resort is an economy all-inclusive type and attracts a lot of European visitors (Two people can stay for somewhere around US $500 for a week). They rent kayaks, snorkel gear, and offer other aquatic activities such as tube rides and more, providing great people-watching opportunities. I relished being able to take my book and lunch to the beach and just wriggle my toes in the sand and, while the weather was hot, I would go as often as possible. With our limited budget, this activity was on my 'free things to do' list. If you go there, just make certain that you do your swimming in the designated swimming areas, as the non-designated areas have numerous short-spined sea urchins ('sea hedgehogs' or 'sea eggs') present on the bottom.

For those of us spending the summer in Luperón, one popular pasttime was America's pasttime (and the Dominican Republic's too) – baseball. The locals were extremely fond of playing softball and it has become a tradition for the cruisers to be invited to participate. We assembled our best

Annie behind the plate.

152

players (actually we assembled anybody and everybody who had any interest in playing) and pitted them against the local team. Of course, since the locals consisted of Luperón's best young talent, to keep things reasonably fair they would lend two or three of their better players to the cruiser team. This made for an interesting matchup and some of the games were reasonably tight. We indulged not only in coed play, but the lady cruisers fielded a women's team to take on the award-winning Luperón women's team. All in all, it was fun for everybody and a great way to get to know the locals.

Tour opportunities were plentiful when we were in Luperón. The local waterfall trip, to Damajagua falls near the town of Imbert, was quite enjoyable and is worth a visit. This trip has the potential to be somewhat dangerous and may not be appropriate for people with serious health issues, mobility problems or weight issues, those with small children, or for those who are lacking in common sense. In addition it probably should not be undertaken after a heavy rain. The best way is to go there as part of a tour, but you can also rent a vehicle and drive yourself and just hire guides once you get there. The guides are necessary to help get you up and through the falls from one level to the next and then back down again. This trip is both wonderfully scenic and lots of fun. Even if you have no intention of climbing the falls, the trip is worthwhile just to see them.

Horseback riding in Luperón is available through Mario's stable. It gave me the chance to see some of the local back country and was quite reasonable. One of my trips took us across the family farm of renowned major league baseball player Sammy Sosa's family.

One way we found to immerse ourselves in the local culture was through cooking classes using the many fruits and vegetables that the DR has to offer. One of the cruisers made arrangements with a local woman, who was interested in opening her own restaurant, to teach a class once a week. These classes were reasonably priced, informative, and fun. Each week she taught us to prepare a different meal and, as a bonus, we got to eat the results of our efforts. The cooking was done outdoors over an open fire or over Cooking classes were fun and tasty. charcoal and was done from scratch without the benefit of any labor-saving ingredients or shortcuts. This was one of our favorite times in Luperón. The recipes that we took with us are still available for us to prepare that ethnic meal when we get the urge and I have included several of them here.

Habichuelas (red beans)

Precook beans til al dente. Will need 30 minutes cooking time to finish.

1 pound	red beans
2 small	onions
1-2 Tbsp	Sazón Ranchero (white)
1-2 Tbsp	vinegar
1	Sour orange, halved, squeezed, and strained

For salsa:
1 tooth (clove) garlic
small handful crushed, minced celery leaves
1 green pepper (aji)
2 Roma type tomatoes, chopped
small handful of fresh cilantro, chopped

Sauté onions in oil until soft. Then add remaining salsa ingredients, except peppers, which go directly into the beans. Sauté all ingredients until well mixed. Then add salsa to beans. Add the Sazón Ranchero, the strained orange juice, and the vinegar and salt to taste.

If you would like another way to take some of the DR's culture with you when you leave, you can sign up for Spanish language lessons at *Captain Steve's Place* in downtown Luperón. Taught by a local schoolteacher, the prices were reasonable.

I (Annie) love to bake and, with our six large opening hatches, we have never had any issues about firing up the oven. While we were anchored in Luperón harbor another boat that we kept meeting up with asked if I would bake for them occasionally as they didn't have a stove or oven on board. It started out with one boat and, as the word got around, I began baking for several boats and also baking bread twice a week for the local yacht club restaurant.

All in all, our stay in the DR was great but after almost eight months, and, even though the record-setting hurricane season was not yet over (unbeknownst to us at the time), it was mid-November and we were ready to move on. We had just spent the longest hurricane season in recorded history (when they actually ran out of names to name them) in the Dominican Republic.

THE *OCEAN WORLD* ALTERNATIVE – On our trip back from Antigua to Florida, in spite of our efforts to avoid the expense and hassle of a stop in the DR, it ended up being more or less unavoidable. As a result, we chose to stop at *Ocean World Marina* near Puerto Plata, rather than Luperón. This allowed us to evaluate the facilities at *Ocean World* and compare them to what we had previously experienced in Luperón.

The *Ocean World Marina* complex is an eyeful when you first enter through the breakwater opening. Located in Cofresi, just west of Puerto Plata, it is a particularly luxurious facility for the Dominican Republic. It was late April, and the marina was all but empty when we were there. Entry to the marina was pretty straightforward, but would probably have been a bit dicey with any kind of a north swell running. Once we got in, the fuel dock was handy and very accessible, even if it was quite high (a convenience for the megayachts which it was built primarily to service).

Ocean World Marina near Puerto Plata, DR

All of the requisite government officials are located right there at the marina and they immediately came to the fuel dock for purposes of checking us in – about as convenient and expeditious a check-in as you might expect to find anywhere. But there was a price to be paid for this speed and convenience.

Amenities provided were of the sort one would expect of a quality facility. When we motored into our slip, dockhands were readily available and seemed competent, and the marina bathroom and shower area was very nice and was well maintained. There was a small dockside store on premises or, had we been so inclined, a courtesy car with driver was available to take us into town for a provisioning trip. In addition we were just a reasonable taxi ride from downtown Puerto Plata had we wanted to undertake anything more involved. We did an engine oil change while alongside here, and there was regular garbage pickup on the dock.

The marina itself is beautiful with a casino located

waterside, and there is a C-shaped swimming pool that wraps around the casino and its first floor poolside dining area. A dip in the swimming pool was really refreshing after having spent several weeks in the tropical heat, first preparing the boat to launch and then sailing her back from Antigua, all without ever taking the time to go for a swim. We elected to eat at the all-you-can-eat dinner buffet that evening and, as is so often the case with these events, it was good but not great.

Expenses at the marina, not surprisingly, seemed a bit on the high side. It cost us about US $150 to check in. We have included in that sum a surcharge of something like fifty dollars charged by the marina, essentially a convenience fee for the officials who are stationed on premises. The marina itself cost us about US $1.65 a foot for the one night we were there. That would amount to $66 a night for a forty foot boat. Electricity and water were available for a nominal fee. Longer term rates came out to about US $4600 for a forty foot boat for a 100 day stay, which might get you most of the way through hurricane season if you got there well into the season. Prior to our departure, the military contingent came in typical DR fashion, and asked for a 'contribution.' We cordially declined, and they dejectedly left.

As a hurricane hole, *Ocean World* just doesn't qualify. It has no protection to speak of other than its location on the north coast of the island. In addition, the surrounding seawall is entirely of rock with little external protection from any surge or seas that might slam into or over it, or those that might curl around through the entrance and into the manmade harbor. *Ocean World Marina* could well be a death trap under such conditions. Luperón harbor would be a much better and safer choice as a hurricane hole.

On the other hand, the protection offered here was adequate for most normal weather and sea states, although I would recommend avoiding entering or leaving in any kind of sizable north swell. It would make an excellent stopover for somebody who wants to stay just a short few days or weeks on their way further down island or when heading back north.

157

Regardless of how whether you choose Luperón or *Ocean World* as your stopover, when sailing the north coast of Hispaniola, it is important to keep a couple of important principals in mind. 1) Make your departure with *no north swell* in the forecast. Any kind of northerly swell tends to make the relatively exposed anchorages untenable along the north coast of the island. This forces you into traveling the entire length of the island. That's not a bad thing if you have an adequate window and it's what you want to do, but you don't want to be forced into it unexpectedly. 2) And, most important of all, leave with a *long* weather window of *light wind from south of east* to allow plenty of time for you to round the eastern tip of Cabo Samaná. Read Bruce's advice on crossing the Mona Passage. 3) If the winds have been blowing steadily for a while, allow an extra day for the seas to lie down before you leave.

Six-pointed starfish

Houses line the shoreline at La Parguera, PR. You can't tell it here but these houses are painted in a variety of beautiful Caribbean pastel colors.

Sancocho (Dominican Stew)   (for 2 people)

1 pound young pork	Peel and cut these
1 pound beef and/or chicken	veggies into pieces:
	3 yuccas
2 Tbsp or more oregano	1 tayote (chayote)
2 tsp salt	½ aujama (yellow squash)
7 medium cloves of garlic	4 carrots
1/4 cup oil	1 ñame
2 limes, juiced	½ yautia
1 sour orange, juiced	4 or 5 green plantains,
sliced	
2 Tbsp Ranchero seasoning	
Bunch of cilantro	
2 small aji gustoso	
½ green pepper	
2 tomatoes (halved and seeded)	
1 small aji	
1 small white onion, quartered	
1 chicken bullion cube	
Water	
Avocados, sliced for garnish	

Cut the meat into chunks and wash in lime juice.
Place oregano, salt, and garlic in mortar and pestle and pulverize

Put cleaned meat into large pot with oil, contents of the mortar and pestle and the lime/orange juice, cover and cook. Add some additional oregano and the Ranchero seasoning on top. Take meat out of pot as it is cooked. Add vegetables to broth and cook, stirring frequently. Mash the yellow squash as it cooks (It gives the broth the golden color). Add the cilantro (to be removed later), the ajis gustosos, and the green pepper, the tomatoes, and cook some more. THE SECRET IS TO STIR IT OFTEN! Remove the vegetables when cooked and return cooked meat to the pot, add the water and onion and bullion cube and cook some more. Return vegetables without the cilantro bundle to pot and cook a bit longer. When all vegetables and meat are completely cooked, serve with sliced avocados on top (if in season).

aji – mild, small banana type) green pepper; aji gustoso is a hot pepper
tayote - chayote
aujama – yellow squash
ñame – a type of yam
yautia – also known as malanga, tannia, tannier, tanier, cocoyam

How About the Dominican Republic?

♦ Pros
  - Excellent storm protection
      - Even 2008 hurricane season with three storms hitting Hispaniola; no significant damage
  - Still get some fronts
  - Huge economy - even if it is third world
      - Can find almost anything you need here
      - Use the DR guidebook portion of Bruce's book to its full advantage here
      - Can be tough to find things here due to language barrier
  - All-inclusive resort just a twenty minute walk from the harbor

♦ Cons - Many people find the DR less than satisfying
  - Local bottled water may be questionable
  - People in Luperón tend to have problem with "the parasite"
  - Not good swimming or diving in the harbor
  - Language issues
      - Carry a Spanish Dictionary
      - Kathy Parson's *Spanish for Cruisers* can be invaluable if you are here for any kind of lengthy stay
  - Constant bickering of the local ex-pats gets old in a hurry
      - Go to one business and you might hear about it from the competition down the street
      - This alone can be significant enough to chase people away

Damajagua Falls near Luperón

After a remarkably good forty-eight hour non-stop crossing from Luperón which took us along the north coast (watch for fish floats anywhere along here) of the DR, around the tip of Cabo Samaná, and then across the Mona Passage, we anchored in Boqueron, on the west coast of Puerto Rico just north of the southwest corner of the island.

Technically you are supposed to bring your vessel into Mayaguez to check in there, but it's a commercial harbor and tends not to be very yacht friendly. Boqueron however, which is only a few miles south, offers a huge, wide open bay and is very easy in and out, so many cruisers choose to bypass Mayaguez.

When we arrived in Boqueron we ran into a friend from Luperón who had arrived the night before and who had a taxi on its way to make the trip into Mayaguez to check in. Our check-in at Mayaguez was routine and we purchased our U.S. Customs sticker which is required in Puerto Rico.

On our way back from checking in, we had the cab driver stop at a grocery store so we could get a turkey to make the next day for Thanksgiving dinner. Our oven aboard *Fidelis* would only accommodate a relatively small turkey (somewhere up to about 16 pounds) but, since we had arrived on the day before Thanksgiving, all of the smaller turkeys were gone. So we bought a duck – outrageously expensive, but tradition is tradition, right?

The next day we had a wonderful Thanksgiving celebration in the cockpit, as three other boats that had arrived from Luperón (*Wounded Spirit*, *Maranatha*, and *Wandering Albatross*) joined us for our feast. We had a full cockpit, a great meal for the holiday, and that little roasted duck, divided eight ways, was the centerpiece of a great feast! We enjoyed ourselves tremendously, not only because we were all extremely happy and thankful finally to be out of the DR and safely across the Mona Passage, but because we were only about 5 miles from the edge of the Caribbean Sea, a major milestone for all of us.

The following day we left Boqueron harbor for nearby Cabo Rojo where we 'turned the corner' onto the south coast of Puerto Rico and into the Caribbean. From Boqueron we moved on to La

Parguera, Guanica, Cayo Aurora (known locally as Gilligan's Island), and then to Ponce. It didn't take us long to get the hang of traveling upwind. Motoring along the south coast of Puerto Rico is much more pleasant and less traumatic when the trade winds are light and/or north of east and when undertaken in the wee hours of the morning (or even at night).

Principals for cruising the south coast of the island of Puerto Rico are the converse of those for doing Hispaniola. Northerly swell is not an issue, since you have the entire island to your north, but occasionally you may have some usually minor swell issues that come more from the south. Your main concern when making your jumps along the southern coast of this island is with wind. Remember to keep it light (preferably under 10 knots) and keep it *north of east*. When you get past the island and out into Vieques Sound, your main concern is simply keeping the breeze *light*.

Downtown Ponce, Puerto Rico

Ponce - The anchorage in Ponce was very small with little swinging room. Not only that, but it was also quite deep. This combination made us uncomfortable to some extent, since we had little confidence in the holding power of our anchor in the event of a wind event.

The boardwalk along the harbor, known by the locals as *la guancha*, was very enjoyable with small food stands lining the walkway. The food prices were reasonable and the foods were tasty. We enjoyed the *pinchos* (grilled meat on a stick - available in a variety of meat and seafood versions) and the *empanadillas* (little meat pies made from a variety of different meats and seafoods). On the weekends there was music, both live and recorded, which blasted the harbor until the wee hours of the morning. Most cruisers couldn't take it for more than a day or so and chose to move on. I think the music may have been related to the holiday season. We hung around because we chose to haul out here and have a bottom job done.

Ponce is Puerto Rico's second largest city. Like most towns along the south coast, it is located on the *autopista* (which is just like any expressway in the U.S.) the principal highway connecting the west coast of the island to San Juan in the northeast. Ponce is also a port of entry.

It was not particularly convenient for us to rent a car here so we chose to walk the two miles or so to the mall where we were able to take in a movie a few times while we were in Ponce. There was also a sizable warehouse type of food store (*Hermanos Santiago Cash and Carry*) just a few short blocks from the harbor. We found a turkey here to take with us to Salinas for Christmas. If you visit this store, don't miss the meat department. It's in a separate room in the back of the store.

We left Ponce and headed for the nearby island of *Caja de Muertos*, or Coffin Island. Here, just five miles away from Ponce, we encountered our first real island snorkeling. The island is a national park. With beds of conch and huge schools of blue tang floating though pristine turquoise water which was host to a plentiful variety of corals, we truly felt that we were finally in the Caribbean. A walk up to the lighthouse at the top of the island offers a breathtaking view of the bay below, the entire island and surrounding ocean, and of Ponce over on the mainland. Be careful though as most of the vegetation is covered with protective thorns or spines of some sort.

Salinas – After a couple days exploring and relaxing in the shadow of *Caja de Muertos* we headed for Salinas, about 20 miles east. We arrived in Salinas on my (Annie) birthday, December 20th. With its spacious, well-protected anchorage, Salinas harbor resembles Luperón. Upon our arrival, we dinghied in to *Marina de Salinas* where, as I was stepping onto the dock

I managed to fall in the water – the old step-on-the-tube-of-the-dinghy-and-the-dinghy-scoots-away-and-*sploosh* routine. Happy birthday to me! In several years of living aboard and three years of constant dock work as I managed the marina in Baltimore, I had seen many a sailor or dockhand take a dive, but I had *never* fallen in the water. It was a humbling experience.

A couple days later, this time with an actual turkey, we celebrated our annual Christmas feast. Once again we were at anchor with *Maranatha*, and *Wounded Spririt*, and this time with one other of our Luperón comrades, Anthony aboard *Aeolus*. Before parting for the last time, we even exchanged token gifts for the occasion.

While in Salinas, you may want to stop in and say hello to Desia at the *Cruiser's Galley* restaurant. When you do, tell her that Annie and Doctor Dave send their regards. She maintains a very cordial, pleasant ambiance and the café is extremely cruiser-friendly. She offers wireless internet on the premises and even out into the bay. There is also a computer room with a number of computer stations, along with good food, beer and drinks, laundry and shower facilities, and other services of value to cruisers.

Marina de Salinas was a *very* cruiser friendly facility with a pleasant staff and a very pleasant, user-friendly laundry. If you choose to anchor out in the bay you can arrange to use the marina swimming pool and showers for a monthly fee. Use of their dinghy dock is free, and gas, diesel, and water are available.

Although the water in Salinas harbor is not particularly pretty, we found Salinas harbor nice enough to swim. The water is dark green from the surrounding mangroves and not terribly attractive but it seems clean enough. We would swim next to the boat quite often and felt comfortable diving to clean the boat bottom as needed. There are resident manatees in the harbor one of which tends be a tad on the friendly side and, when we first arrived there, one of the cows had a recently newborn calf.

Puerto Rico offers some of the biggest bargains you will find in the northern Caribbean, and Salinas provides a convenient central location from which to take advantage of everything. Salinas is an excellent place to rent a car. You can call *Timely Car Rental* in nearby Santa Isabel or call the local *Hertz* agency right in Salinas and have a car delivered right to the marina. Just tell them where you are, when you need it and for how long, and either agency will pick you up, and when you return the car they will bring you back. Cost, last thing we knew, was about $35.00 for 24 hours.

From Salinas you can head in either direction. There is a *Sam's Club* in Ponce and another in Caguas up near San Juan. In Caguas, in the same shopping center with the *Sam's Club,* there is also a *Costco*. Wherever you are in the country you can just rent a car for the day to get there. These places are accessible from all over Puerto Rico and, by ferry and a rental car for the day, from Culebra and Vieques in the Spanish Virgins.

We are big movie buffs. We enjoy a trip to the movies and a big tub of popcorn. There are a couple of large cineplexes in Ponce that are convenient and easy to get to by rental car. We would have the rental car people drop off the car in the morning, take the *autopista* to San Juan and/or Ponce (Ponce is about 30 miles west and San Juan is about 45 miles to the northeast.) for the day, come back to the marina and unload our goodies into the dinghy and run them out to the boat. If necessary we would borrow one of the marina's wagons to get our stuff from car to dinghy. Then we would pile back into the car and drive to Ponce (or sometimes Caguas) for a movie. *Caribbean Cinemas* offers senior citizen discounts to those 50 years or older, so we even got a break on the movie prices. With many of the movies you must pay attention as to whether it is in Spanish or in English if it matters to you. Those movies that are in English will often be subtitled. We saw previews for some really funny Puerto Rican movies that unfortunately for us were released only in Spanish without subtitles. Our Spanish just isn't that good.

We did most of our provisioning in Caguas, which is about 10 miles before San Juan and has, in addition to the *Sam's Club* and *Costco*, a *Pep Boys*, *Super Wal-Mart*, *Pueblo* (major grocery chain), and a *K-Mart* all virtually in the same place. Across town there is a *Home Depot*. AND best of all, there's a *Caribbean Cinema* right next to the *Home Depot*.

In Salinas harbor, *Playa Marine*, a chandlery located just a short walk from *Marina de Salinas*, was one of the most complete marine stores we encountered on our trip. They carry a vast array of marine and boating supplies comparable to a smaller *West Marine* or *Budget Marine* store. Prices are comparable to the major chains' list prices and the staff is friendly and helpful. If for some reason you must have a *West Marine*, there are two of them in Puerto Rico. One is in downtown San Juan only a few blocks away from the *Plaza de las Americas*, a huge indoor mall, and the other is on the east coast at Fajardo.

Ponce offers most of your major chain stores including *Sears*, *Wal-Mart*, and much more but shopping there is not near as convenient as in Caguas. Near Salinas, in Santa Isabel just up the street from *Timely Car Rental*, there is a *Super Wal-Mart* with great prices on food and supplies. And in Salinas itself there are two *Amigo* grocery stores, the other major Puerto Rican grocery store chain.

Although the mangroves are not as large as one might ideally choose, the hurricane hole at Jobos is worthy of consideration in the event of an oncoming storm. Check it out! (But we were warned not to swim there – contaminated water.)

Because of all that it has to offer, and because of its convenient location in the middle of the south coast of Puerto Rico, right on the northern border of the Caribbean, Salinas is a popular summertime hurricane hole (The well-sheltered hurricane hole at Jobos, is only 3 miles east of Salinas harbor.) and a popular provisioning destination for cruisers throughout the eastern and northern Caribbean. We were in and out of Salinas a number of times on our trip.

Salinas is the final protected jumping off point for the Virgin

Islands. You can knock four or five miles off the trip by staging out to *Boca del Infierno* for an early morning start. Although some folks are quite intimidated by starting their passage by jumping through the 'mouth of hell,' this 200 yard opening can be carefully navigated, even in the dark, if the weather is settled. Just make sure that you are several hundred yards past the opening before you make your swing to the east.

HEADS-UP! Along the south coast of Puerto Rico, from Boca del Inferno eastward almost to Puerto Patillas, watch for fish floats, particularly along the highly touted '10-fathom trench.'

When sailing in the dark along this route we tried to stay 3 to 5 miles off shore to avoid an extended zone of fish floats that lie roughly along and also well-inside the 100 foot bottom contour. The first time we traveled from Salinas to Culebra, we chose to stop in the afternoon and drop anchor along the shore at Isabel II (*Isabel Segundo*) on the north shore of the island of Vieques. This is a reasonable stop if you have light breezes and no northerly swell and it lies only about eight miles or so from Culebra and only about twenty miles from St. Thomas.

Looking back at the lift bridge from the canal in Dewey, Culebra, PR. Evidently this bridge is not operational.

Finally, What About Puerto Rico?

♦ Pros
- Most of the upside of the Dominican Republic
- Reasonable storm protection here; but remember you're on a *south* coast exposure
- Language is still Spanish
- But there is always someone close by who speaks English
- All of the pluses of being in the United States
- Cheap plane flights to the U.S.
- None of the downside of the third world here
- Can find anything you might need
- You are in the Caribbean here
- Popular as a 'home base' even for cruisers who are in the southern Caribbean

Salinas harbor, Puerto Rico – a very pleasant harbor to visit – good protection, good holding, friendly people.

Culebra, one of the so-called Spanish Virgin Islands, was one of my (Annie) all-time favorite places to be. In Culebra we would anchor out in *Bahía Honda*, the large bay that fronts up against the main village of Dewey, or we would grab a free mooring out in Dakity Bay, a couple miles from town, and we would dinghy the length of *Bahía Honda* into Dewey.

Culebra offers some areas that are quite well-protected by mangroves should you need storm protection. In addition there is a good-sized, very accessible anchorage right near Dewey, and several mooring fields at various locations around the island which are provided by the Puerto Rican natural resources department – and the moorings as of 2007 were still FREE!

NOTE: Always dive and check your mooring in Puerto Rican waters. They are excellent moorings but they get a lot of use and not a lot of maintenance.

Just be sure you always dive your mooring and check its condition. On weekends and holidays when the weather is nice, the locals have a tendency to come out in droves in large, powered cabin cruisers and, in order to enjoy the trade wind breeze blowing in through their stern cabin entryways, they tie up stern-to to the moorings. Then another two or three (or more) large cruisers will often raft alongside, also presenting their huge aft exposures to the trade winds. Needless to say this fleet provides a lot of wear and tear to the mooring lines, not to mention the sand screws to which they are attached. It is not unusual to find the screw pulled two or three feet out of the sand and bent over at a ninety degree angle. So check.

We loved the blue-green water of Dakity Bay where we hung out for extended periods of time swimming, snorkeling over a huge bed of sea cucumbers and large starfish, and just kicking back. The bay, which is on the south shore of Culebra, is protected by a surrounding barrier reef on three sides which gives you the sensation of being anchored out in very open water. Yet the surrounding reef provides excellent wave protection in all weather up to mild storm conditions.

Sometimes, for entertainment while snorkeling, we would have starfish races. Turn over two or more starfish and then float on the surface and watch them slowly turn back over. It was interesting how they did it, and surprising the differences in the speed with which they could turn themselves.

From downtown Dewey we would catch the ferry to Fajardo on the Puerto Rican mainland, one of the best deals in the islands, thanks probably to substantial subsidies from American taxpayers. You can ride the hour long, seventeen mile ferry ride for about $3.00 per person each way. On a beautiful sunny day this little trip is entertainment in its own right. On one trip we observed a breaching whale not far from the ferry.

Just like in Salinas, we would rent a car for around $35.00 for the day and hit all of the local provisioning stops, including a large *Pueblo* grocery, *Wal-Mart* and *K-Mart*, the local *West Marine* store, *Pep Boys*, and more. If you need to make a run to *Sam's Club*, there is one located not far from Fajardo in Carolina, on the highway to San Juan. Just make certain you're back in time for the last ferry back to Culebra in the late afternoon – and make sure you don't accidentally get the ferry to Vieques by mistake.

While on one of our trips to the *Pueblo* grocery store, we coincidentally happened to meet up with a Brazilian couple, Bob and Isabel of the sloop *Bicho Vermelho*, whom we had met once before, if only briefly, about five years earlier while we were anchored in Annapolis, Maryland. It had been one of those curiosity stops as we were dinghying past a Brazilian boat and simply decided to stop briefly and say 'hi.' They invited us aboard for a quick chat and that was it. Unbelievably I (David) recognized them in the *Pueblo* store in Fajardo and we struck up a conversation. Another brief encounter, we ended up giving them and their purchases a ride back to their boat aboard which they were en route to Venezuela.

View of St. Thomas from atop Culebrita in the Spanish Virgin Islands.

In addition to car rentals, we also learned to use the *publico* system in Puerto Rico. It is similar to the network of *gua-guas* used by the locals in the Dominican Republic, however it can be more frustrating. In Puerto Rico, if you are not careful, your fixed-fare *publico* can suddenly turn into a full-priced taxi ride if you don't make arrangements in advance. On visits from Culebra to Fajardo you can hire a *publico* at the ferry dock to take you where you need to go. Check the price first and find out where you can get picked up for the trip back. And, just like in the DR, if you should happen to take a *publico*, try to check with someone else who is riding in order to find out what they are paying. If you look like a tourist there will be a tendency for your fare to inflate. You can also generally find a local *publico* stop in most small towns, often located inside a parking ramp.

Once while we were in Culebra we decided to fly from San Juan back to Florida on business. To avoid the expense of a taxi from Fajardo to the airport, about 30 miles or so, we decided to take a *publico*. A few days prior to our departure we enjoyed one of our shoreside adventures as we made a practice *publico* run from Fajardo to Rio Piedras, where we transferred to a San Juan metro bus for the second leg to the airport. It's not easy to do, but it saved us enough money over the cost of a taxi to allow us to spend a relaxing night before our flight at a hotel near the airport.

Culebra has a very laid back feel with a great little airport, plenty of restaurants, and even some night life. The local food, such as that offered by the *Dinghy Dock* bar and restaurant near the canal in downtown Dewey, where they offer both pretty decent tourist food and local fare at reasonable prices, is excellent, but there is also more. Among other eateries, we encountered a couple from Maryland who had moved there and opened a small bar/restaurant on the way to the airport. The owner, who hails from Maryland, imports her crab and makes genuine Maryland crab cakes that are excellent.

Just a short sail from Culebra is the nearby island of Culebrita where you can find excellent snorkeling in everything from shallow to relatively deep water. This was some of the best snorkeling that we found on our trip. We were able to anchor the boat in a large sand patch and, when the boat drifted back on the breeze, we were suspended over beautiful coral about 20 feet beneath the boat without our anchor chain contacting any coral. David was able to spear three good-sized fish, a flounder, a jack, and a porgy one day in a matter of a couple of hours. We snorkeled among hawksbill and green turtles here and saw those huge schools of blue tang that we so enjoy. We were anchored off the western shore of Culebrita and, with a mild north swell running, were able to lie comfortably to an anchor bridle.

We took the dinghy ashore and went exploring. There is a very pleasant sandy beach here where we did some beachcombing and swimming. We also walked to the top of the island to check out the abandoned lighthouse. From there we were able to peer down into *Bahía Tortuga* (Turtle Bay) to the north with its numerous mooring balls and over at nearby St. Thomas, about 15 miles to the east.

Puerto Rico's Spanish Virgins (which include Culebra and Vieques and a number of smaller islands to the west known collectively as *la Cordillera*) offer pristine water with great snorkeling, diving, and fishing, plus no-cost moorings – you can't get much better than that! They are wonderful, inexpensive, and not very crowded (other than on those weekends we just mentioned). Most cruisers, if they stop at all on their quest to reach St. Thomas and 'the Caribbean,' stop for only a day or two. So for good quality, economical cruising, and time away from the madding crowd, keep this region in mind.

At some point you will decide to head over to the USVI. When we were there it was not necessary to check into the USVI upon arrival when coming from Puerto Rico. Puerto Rico though does require that you check in when coming from the USVI. And if you decide to travel back and forth between the USVI and Puerto Rico more than once, sign up for the U.S. Customs Local Boat Option (LBO) program which will allow you to check in with a simple phone call and a registration number without the need for repeatedly visiting the customs office when checking in and out of the U.S. and its possessions.

Free moorings abound in the Spanish Virgin Islands of Puerto Rico. This is Bahía Moldovar in Culebra.

Shoreside in Christmas Cove, Great St. James, Island, USVI

On our first pass through the U.S. Virgins we had expected to make a brief stop and just move on. We had been to the USVI a number of times in the past and had never been terribly impressed. We were anticipating the hustle and bustle of the big city and a palpable feeling of oppression from the crowds. And, in truth, you can get that when you are on the streets of downtown Charlotte Amalie or visiting area shopping or tourist destinations. However, aboard a vessel anchored in one of the nearby anchorages, there is something of a sense of removal from all of that.

St. Thomas – We found that St. Thomas harbor offered us a stark contrast to the quiet, serene setting of Culebra, and we actually caught ourselves enjoying watching the people, the cruise ships, and all of the associated activity there. In other words, for short periods of time it was a fun place to visit.

We have anchored in numerous places around Charlotte Amalie. Druif Bay (known among cruisers as Honeymoon Bay) is a small, crowded anchorage located in the lee of Water Island. Because of the limited space, we elected to anchor on the outer edge of the bay in over 30 feet of water. The bottom of Honeymoon Bay is littered with a variety of junk and debris from past storms and with old moorings. We are uncomfortable anchoring on a foul bottom so we didn't spend much time there. They offer some great hamburgers at the little beach food stand here.

Elephant Bay, also on the west shore of Water Island and a tad north of Druif Bay, lies just across the West Gregerie Channel from Crown Bay with its marina and cruise ship docks. Crown Bay Marina has an excellent marine store (*Island Marine*) and a nice laundromat where we were able to get free wi-fi.

The protection offered by the anchorages on the west side of Water Island is quite good under prevailing conditions. It's reasonably convenient to town, very little swell works its way in and, other than the occasional wake and the large number of unoccupied (read derelict) boats anchored there, it's not a bad place.

We have also anchored a number of times in the area of the West Indian Company cruise ship dock (at Havensight) on Long Bay in St. Thomas harbor proper. This is the main cruise ship dock for the downtown area. This anchorage is a little more exposed to the effects of swell and can get a little rolly at times. Because of its proximity to the heart of downtown Charlotte Amalie and the easy access to the local bus (VITRAN - Virgin Islands Transportation) system, we stayed here quite often. When we were there, a brand new marina had just opened adjacent to the Havensight cruise ship dock. If offered a variety of facilities and it is our understanding that a new *Budget Marine* store has now opened up there.

In St. Thomas we found another *PriceSmart* store (even better than the one in Santiago in the DR) and another similar type store just up the road called *Cost-U-Less*. Both places are a dollar (not $2, as some of the local dollar taxi drivers will try to charge you) taxi ride from the main harbor by the Coast Guard station in St. Thomas. There is a *Caribbean Cinemas* cineplex and a *Home Depot* in the same little center with the *Cost-U-Less* store. We would load up with groceries at *Cost-U-Less*, then walk over to the movies where the employees would very kindly allow us to stash our carts full of goodies in a storeroom while we would take in a movie before heading back to the harbor.

One peculiarity we noticed while anchored in Long Bay where downtown Charlotte Amalie is close by – they have an overabundance of siren traffic for such a small town. It seems that all day long, and sometimes well into the night, every vehicle with a siren turns it on when traveling along the waterfront, evidently in an effort to speed up their trip through the constant standstill of bumper-to-bumper traffic. A city this size simply can't have that many emergencies, unless going to lunch and going home from work constitute emergencies.

There is a bus stop and a place where you can stop a taxi right beside the downtown dinghy dock. *Home Depot*, *Price-Smart*, *Cost-U-Less*, and the *Caribbean Cinema* are just a bus ride or a dollar taxi ride from downtown. Just like at home, the buses have fixed bus stops. When catching a dollar taxi, you stand beside the street and flag it down, then simply buzz the driver to indicate where you want to get off.

There are two types of taxis in St. Thomas, regular taxis, which will go pretty much anywhere you want, and the 'dollar taxi.' You will find taxis that are automobiles just like you are used to at home, but also some that are taxi buses which look like open-air jitneys – a pickup truck type body with several rows of bench type seats in the back covered by a large awning. The regular taxis cater to the tourists and cruise ship patrons and they charge typical taxi prices which can be much more costly. The 'dollar taxis' follow a fixed route similar to the bus system and they charge by zones. Most places that you might want to go are only a dollar ride away from downtown. All 'dollar taxis' (as far as we could see) are open air taxi buses - BUT all open air taxi buses are NOT necessarily 'dollar taxis.'

If you go to the Mandela Mall or beyond there toward Red Hook, it is a two-dollar ride. Anything closer than that fell into the one dollar zone. (With the price of gas climbing as it has, these prices may very well increase.)

When you climb aboard, stop and tell the driver where you are going and ask how much it will cost to get there. That way there won't be any surprises. The price when you come back should be the same. If you have any doubts, while you are riding ask the locals what they are paying and/or what you should be paying. It should be the same price they pay. We had at least one incident of a driver trying to charge us incorrectly just because she could tell we were not locals. Even the locals with whom we were riding came to our defense when we refused to pay the inflated charges. So remember that occasionally the drivers will charge you by who you appear to be, not by where you are going.

If you want to avoid hassles, just catch a bus at the VITRAN bus stop. These are plain old city type buses and they don't care who you are or where you're going. Their prices are fixed and you can ride all over the island. Since they run a fixed schedule, they just aren't quite as convenient or plentiful.

By the way, if you have not been there before, remember that throughout the Virgin Islands, both U.S. and British, vehicles drive on the left side of the road. It can be difficult (and fatal) to adjust to looking first to the right instead of the left when you cross the street. And don't get careless. In St. Thomas, you might as well be in Manhattan. The drivers don't cut you any slack.

A couple miles east of the eastern end of St. Thomas are the St. James Islands – Great St. James and Little St. James – the back sides of which contribute to the western shoreline of Pillsbury Sound, the body of water that separates St. Thomas from St. John. Located on the wester side, in the lee of Great St. James Island is Christmas Cove, one of our favorite anchorages in the USVI. It's a large cove that is wide open to the west, it is quite well protected under most prevailing conditions, and it's popular among both cruisers and local commercial charter groups. It is a reasonable dinghy ride from Red Hook Bay on the east end of St. Thomas, but we found the trip into Red Hook by dinghy just a little too rough, a little too hectic, and a little too wet with the constant ferry traffic from St. Thomas to both the BVI and St. John. We got soaked the couple of times we made the trip.

Christmas Cove is well-removed from the commotion of St. Thomas harbor. But some cruisers find the occasional wakes from the continuous passing of large power boats and ferries through adjacent Current Cut, which connects the waters of St. James Bay to those of Pillsbury Sound, to be annoying. Others are bothered by the 'cattle boats,' both power and sail, which bring in herds of snorkelers most days for a few hours at a time on day trips from the cruise ships. We thought it was a hoot. We found ourselves amused and entertained by the charter skippers and their daytrippers. And with our big heavy hull, we felt that the wakes, which seldom occurred past sunset, were usually not an issue.

One of the reasons that this location is popular among the day excursion boats is the above average snorkeling that it offers, combined with its relatively close proximity to the cruise ship docks in St. Thomas. Even just sitting in the cockpit and relaxing, it was not at all unusual for a large manta ray to come soaring through the water beneath the anchored boat, wings undulating slowly as it passed. On more than one occasion we saw a huge, forty pound grouper cruise by and this was one of the only locations where we encountered a moray eel, living in the rocks as we snorkeled near shore.

We loved the snorkeling and the people-watching in Christmas Cove and returned there several times. Not only does it make for a fun anchorage in its own right for a couple of days, but it makes a great stopover when traversing between St. Thomas and the islands of the BVI

St. John – While in the USVI we spent about three weeks anchored over in St. John in Coral Bay, one of the few locations in St. John where you are allowed to anchor and therefore do not have to pay for a mooring ball. Coral Bay is located on the east end of St. John and is a huge bay most of which is wide open to the south. Since we were on a limited budget, with the exception of the time we spent in Coral Bay our time in St. John was limited.

At the time we were trying to sort out a problem with our watermaker and the local rep was located in Cruz Bay. To do our shopping we would catch the VITRAN bus from Coral Bay across the island into Cruz Bay, catch the ferry from there over to Red Hook on St. Thomas, then take the bus or a dollar taxi from there to *Cost-U-Less* and/or *PriceSmart*. This would tie up an entire day, which was always a fun and sometimes frustrating adventure.

St. John – Maho Bay – This was one of the many bays on St. John where anchoring is not permitted. In these locations you must pay $25 a night for a mooring ball. Payment may be on the honor system. Make sure you pay for your mooring. You do not want to hear your boat named on the VHF radio as one of those who have sneaked off without paying.

In 2006 as Christmas season approached and we were

hanging out in Culebra, we decided to visit the USVI for the holidays. While we were there we happened to overhear our friends Chuck and Terri of *Maker's Match* calling somebody on the radio. We had not seen Chuck and Terri since our hurricane holeup back in Luperón and we were eager to get together with them. We contacted them and found that they and some other mutual friends from our old DR crowd, along with some friends of theirs that we had never met, were going to be getting together in Maho Bay on St. John for a traditional group Christmas dinner on the beach. We prepared a sixteen pound turkey with stuffing and a rum cake, *Maker's Match* brought a pineapple casserole, *Pirates Hideaway* made mashed potatoes, and *Serendipity* (Pam and Jeff and the girls, still with cat Whiskers and Beagle dog Buddy, more friends from the DR) made pumpkin pies. Other boats, including our Luperón friends Steve and Sue aboard their new cat *Evensong*, brought brownies, salads, and more casseroles. We had one of the best Christmas dinners we have ever had, complete with an after-dinner caroling session with David playing guitar and everyone joining in the singing.

Celebrating Christmas on the beach – Maho Bay, St. John, USVI

Many cruisers labor under the impression that the BVI no longer has anything to offer for the liveaboard cruiser. We certainly felt that way. Rumors abound about the overwhelming numbers of charter boats and the anchorages that have been filled with mooring balls placed their for the benefit of those charter boats. We spent nearly three weeks cruising the BVI late in the spring and did not have to take a mooring ball any of those nights.

A leisurely daysail from Christmas Cove in the USVI took us to Great Harbour on Jost Van Dyke where we did our BVI check-in. Check-in was simple and straightforward. In the British Virgins, fees for a short visit of less than thirty days are quite reasonable – generally less than ten dollars. To stay longer than a month however, you are required to pay a tax that amounts to several hundred dollars on an average boat. This has a tendency to curb most people's urge to stay any longer than the initial 30 days.

No trip to Jost Van Dyke is complete without a trip to Foxy's

Although most of the really popular anchorages in the BVI are full of mooring balls, Great Harbour was one location where, in spite of an abundance of charter boats, there were no moorings. It is important to be vigilant when anchoring among the charterers if they are not on moorings, since some charterers are quite inept when anchoring (certainly *not all*, by any means – although we certainly fell into the 'anchoring impaired' category years ago when we chartered in the BVI), which explains the tendency for the most popular anchorages to be filled with moorings.

From Great Harbour we sailed over to Cane Garden Bay where we anchored out beyond the few moorings that are there and still enjoyed the protection of the outlying reef. Cane Garden is one of the most picturesque bays in the BVI with a beautiful palm-lined, crescent beach. It offers several small shops along with a number of resorts and some nightlife.

After a couple of days in Cane Garden Bay we headed along the north shore of Tortola, nosing into Brewers Bay to have a peak from a distance at the old camp ground where we used to go camping for a couple weeks or more each winter before our sailing days began. Our daysail ended when we dropped the hook in White Bay, actually more of a small bight than a real bay, on the south shore of Guana Island.

From Guana Island we moseyed over and around Great Camanoe Island to Marina Cay where we anchored in a small bay on the edge of Great Camanoe a few hundred yards from the Pussers resort. Here, surprisingly, we were able to utilize their free wifi. The holding in this little cove was tenuous at best. In spite of our efforts to hand-set the anchor, we were unable to back it down adequately and we spent a quiet but restless night.

From Marina Cay we decided to head over toward Virgin Gorda. We were heading toward Little Dix Bay on the northwestern shoreline of the island and, as we were approaching we decided that the guidebook description of neighboring Savannah Bay sounded really interesting. Although the entrance was just a little bit challenging, this anchorage turned out to be our favorite of the entire BVI trip and we ended up staying there for several days.

The outlying reef at Savannah Bay is an effective barrier to many sailboats trying to enter the bay and requires that you enter and exit by passing quite close to the shoreline at the southwestern end of the bay. Once you are safely past the reef there is a large 'X' painted on the rocks ashore at which point you can turn and parallel the shoreline. This bay is essentially wide open to the northwest with the outlying reef offering nothing in the way of protection from any northerly swell. As a result, this is not a particularly viable anchorage during the winter months. Most nights during our stay we were the only boat anchored here.

With a beautiful, mile long, crescent shaped sandy beach, nearly devoid of people, and lined with palm trees, Savannah Bay has to be one of the most beautiful beaches in the world. The bay itself offers snorkeling at a variety of depths. We were able to anchor in about 10 feet of water over a wide open sandy bottom and dropped back into 20 feet of crystalline beauty. Right underneath our boat we found sand dollars so plentiful that we ended up with 20 or 30 perfect specimens, while almost immediately behind the boat was a twenty-five or thirty foot deep coral reef with acres of fan coral. When we snorkeled this deep reef it became shallower and shallower again as we moved further out from shore.

In nearer to shore and to the east of us was what must be an ancient stand of giant elkhorn coral, featuring younger elkhorn coral growing on top of older elkhorn. This reef reached from a hundred yards or more from shore virtually all the way to the shoreline. It was so thick that there was no way to swim through it and it extended from the bottom all the way to the surface of the water. The diversity of the fish here and their apparent lack of shyness, as with most reef diving in the BVI, was extraordinary. This is likely attributable to the nearly universal ban on spearfishing there. Savannah Bay is remembered by both of us as one of the high points of our Caribbean experience.

One of the days while we were anchored in Savannah Bay we decided to take the dinghy for a ride past neighboring Little Dix Bay and over to Spanish Town, about two miles away, to fill a couple of our gerry jugs with fuel. The marina in Spanish Town was quite nice, with a pleasant shopping complex containing not only a grocery store but also an ice cream shop, and the ride over and back wasn't bad.

From Savannah Bay we started to wend our way back toward the U.S. Virgins. We headed over toward Cooper Island to check out the anchorage there but were unable to find anything with which we felt comfortable, because of the depth of the water and the extent of the mooring field. Rather than spend a night having to watch over our anchor, we chose to sail across to Fat Hogs Bay on the southern shoreline of Tortola.

Years ago we had done our first ever charter through SeaBreeze charters which was headquartered in Fat Hogs Bay. The now-abandoned facility there was in a rather sad state of disrepair and neglect. Fat Hogs Bay was disappointing. The water was so cloudy that I had to dive our anchor and examine it by feel rather than visually. As a result we headed out first thing the next morning.

Our daysail this time was just a simple motor trip around Buck Island and over to neighboring Maya Cove. Maya Cove was beautiful, with the expected pristine BVI water and a nice sandy bottom with excellent holding. Although there was nothing there to keep us, the anchorage was just pleasantly active enough to keep us entertained and we ended up staying for more than just a single overnight. It was right outside the harbor where *Sunsail* charters has their home base, and the continuous coming and going of the charter boats made for some great people watching. Plus, with the 'if it's Tuesday, this must be Jost Van Dyke' charter mentality, we did not have to be concerned about the *Sunsail* charter boats anchoring here. They were in too big a hurry to get to the first day's stop or to get their boat back to its berth and head for home.

From Maya Cove we decided that our BVI visit would just

not be complete without a visit to Road Town. We dropped the hook on the west side of Road Bay not far from the ferry docks. From there we decided to take our dinghy and motor over to "nearby" Nanny Cay. We had bought *Fidelis* at Nanny Cay many years ago and just wanted to have a look around. The trip to Nanny Cay by dinghy was one of the stupidest things we managed to do in our entire cruise. It was about three miles from where we anchored and required that we traverse the breadth of wide open Sea Cow Bay in our eleven foot inflatable. The trip across to Nanny Cay was quite unpleasant but, a few hours later, the upwind trip back to Road Harbour was absolutely miserable. We spent another day anchored on the east side of Road Bay, off what is commonly referred to as the old CSY charter base, in Baugher's Bay. From there we dinghied into town and wandered around Road Town for the day.

After a few weeks of cruising the BVI, it was time for our departure. Since our middle daughter, Jennifer, is married to a Thornton and we have three grandchildren with the Thornton surname, we felt that we could not leave the BVI without paying homage to the world-famous Willie T (the *William Thornton*). Although the vessel is barely worthy of the term 'boat,' and the food can be marginal, we enjoyed our visit there and picked up t-shirts for our daughter and her husband. Located in the bight on the north shore of Norman Island, this was our one concession to the ready availability of a commercial mooring (US $18.00 for the night), since our plan was to leave first thing in the morning to head back to Christmas Cove in the USVI. We did find that, had we been so inclined, there was some space to anchor in shallow water in the western corner of the bay near the shoreline.

We enjoyed the northern Caribbean a great deal – so much so that we really had no great interest in crossing the Anegada passage and heading southward through the Leeward Islands. The readily available remoteness and quietude of the Spanish Virgin Islands, combined with the easy access to common American conveniences and provisioning in St. Thomas and especially

View of Cane Garden Bay on Tortola, BVI

Puerto Rico, made us reluctant to leave it all behind. We had enjoyed all of the amenities of U.S. coastal cruising yet we were doing it in paradise! Had it not been for an invitation from our friends MaryLiz and Chris aboard *Wandering Albatross* to join them as crew aboard their Westsail 32 in the Antigua Classic Yacht Regatta, we would probably have continued to hang out in the Virgins. As it was, in spite of a very limited amount of racing experience, we decided this was an invite we couldn't pass up.

As the time to leave approached, we staged out from Christmas Cove to Maho Bay on St. John where we picked up a mooring. This would allow us an early departure without the need for picking up an anchor and all of the associated rigamarole. Most people elect to go first to the BVI and then cross from there. However, for us the weather windows at this time were very spotty and unpredictable and we wanted to keep our options open. We did not want the inconvenience and expense of having to check in and then check out and then possibly check in again (paying each time), if for some reason we decided to change our minds. We figured that, if the weather didn't pan out we would simply turn the trip into an extended daysail, or we might even decide to cruise the BVI for a week or two while waiting for weather.

As it turned out, we departed the very next morning and did an eight hour daysail up the Drake Channel through the BVI on a beautiful, cloudless day with a gentle breeze – just what we were looking for. It gave us ample opportunity to evaluate the weather and decide if it was what we wanted, prior to actually jumping out into the Sombrero (Anegada) Passage. That evening, as the sun was setting in the west, Virgin Gorda and Cooper Island were just sinking beneath the horizon as we motorsailed quietly along. Our crossing was perfect – uneventful, quiet, no wind, and minimal seas – just an easy upwind motorsail across a potentially very uncomfortable piece of water. We arrived off Simpson Bay, St. Maarten at dawn the next morning rested and ready to go.

This pelican makes a pleasant rest stop for the gull.

Customs and immigration office (*Gare Maritime*) in Marigot, French
St. Martin

Upon our arrival in St. Martin, we anchored in Simpson Bay on the Dutch side and dinghied in to the customs house, which is located right next to the bridge, to check in. The official check-in routine is not terribly expensive in either country, but if you intend to stay for a while the French side is considerably cheaper. And, once you have checked in, even though you are *supposed to* check in and out when you move from one side to the other, you can easily move back and forth at will.

In Simpson Bay (Dutch side), we anchored relatively close to the beach on the north side of the bay. This bay, which opens to the southwest, is about a mile and a half across at its mouth and about a mile deep with a beautiful, sandy beach extending for about 130° around it. The beach is lined with beach houses and small rental properties and is really popular for sunbathing among the tourists. I (Annie) loved to take the dinghy ashore here and walk the beach. You need to be aware though that the bottom drops off quite quickly when you step off the beach.

In St. Martin we once again caught up with good friends Chuck and Terri, and boat dog Vince, of *Maker's Match*, who we had not seen since Christmas. They had taken off, crossing from the Virgins, several weeks before us and, like us, were on their way to Antigua to meet up with *Wandering Albatross*.

For most of our time on the Dutch side, if the weather was settled we chose to remain anchored out in Simpson Bay and dinghy in from there if need be. We would go inside and anchor in the large Simpson Bay Lagoon if the bay got rolly or if we had projects to do, as the stores were much more accessible from there. The lagoon is huge, about 3 miles long by a mile or more across in some areas. You can enter the lagoon through either bridge, the new large bascule bridge on the Dutch end or via the smaller, older one on the French side.

When on the Dutch side we spent a substantial amount of time at *Shrimpy's* restaurant and bar where he offered a sailor's flea market every Sunday morning along with free draft beer for as long as the keg held out. He also offered free wi-fi and, as a former cruiser himself, made every effort to make his establishment cruiser-friendly. Stop in and have a beer and order some food. This kind of place needs the patronage of cruisers if it is to survive and flourish. His meat and seafood pies are excellent.

Simpson Bay Lagoon, Dutch Sint Maarten

Since Sint Maarten is home to a sizable fleet of megayachts, there are lots of warehouse type stores where you can provision. You just have to ask around and search for them. Most are located over in the neighborhood around Cole Bay, at the southeast corner of the lagoon on the northeast shore near most of the marine facilities. Here you will also find two large marine stores, *Budget Marine* and *Island Water World*, the two major chandlery chains that are located throughout the Caribbean. These stores are really quite big and, because St. Maarten is duty free, you can find some of the best equipment and supply bargains in the islands. Along the shoreline of Cole Bay and in the adjacent neighborhood you will also find a variety of machine shops, electrical shops, riggers, sailmakers, and any other type of marine specialist you might need or want. Plus, there is also a cinema nearby.

We bought a brand new yellow hard bottom inflatable

Caribe brand dinghy from *Island Water World* for under $2000. The same dinghy is $3000 here in the U.S. We liked it better than any other brands we saw and, between the generous inventories of two large marine stores, the available selection was impressive.

As we have mentioned, wherever we travel we prefer to take buses as our preferred means of transportation if possible. The bus system in St. Martin is user-friendly and we rode it several times into downtown Philipsburg where there was a *Cost-U-Less* store similar to the one in St. Thomas. Prices at this store (as in most stores on the Dutch side) are in guilders (standard currency of the Netherlands Antilles), the standard currency of Sint Maarten, so you need to know the exchange rate when you provision at these stores.

There is also a casino in the Cole Bay area where we went and played a few times. It has a dinghy dock nearby where you can tie up and just walk up to the casino. They featured a Texas Hold'em tournament every Sunday night and some friends of ours went and participated. We had some fun at the casinos in Sint Maarten and, because our budget was limited, our losses were too (and our winnings even moreso).

The beach at Grand Case, French St. Martin.

In Marigot there are lots of little French restaurants and we found great buys on inexpensive French wine. My (Annie) favorite thing here was the bakeries (patisseries) with their lovely baguettes and their fresh, hot croissants at breakfast whenever we wanted to indulge. Downtown Marigot has an open air market that runs along the waterfront. The sellers fly in from Guadeloupe with their wares – spices, fruits, plants, baked goods, clothes, and crafts.

We sailed around the west and northwest sides of St. Martin to several ports, including Grand Case, where they have the largest concentration of French restaurants on the island. One night each week during the tourist season they have a street festival where they block off the main street to vehicular traffic and the street is filled with vendors selling their crafts and visitors enjoying the sights, sounds, and taste of French St. Martin. The Eurodollar is the standard of currency on the French side of the island, and even though the exchange rate was close to two to one, many of the restaurants offered special one to one deals in order to get the American dollars.

We also stopped in at some of the other smaller ports along this part of the island as we sailed out to Ile Tintamarre and back. Ile Tintamarre is a small island with a very colorful history, located off the northwest corner of St. Martin. The island offers beautiful scenery, a spectacular beach and anchorage, and the opportunity for visitors to enjoy a free body masque utilizing the mud available above the beach on this island, a mud which supposedly has special dermatological properties.

St. Martin race week took place while we were there. This is one of the premier regatta events in the Caribbean racing circuit with racing teams and their yachts arriving from all over the world. If you enjoy peace and quiet and tranquility, then this week is probably not the week you want to be there. We chose this week to make our move from Simpson Bay on the Dutch side to Marigot Bay on the French side. We had prepared ourselves and our vessel to depart early in the morning the following day. However around mid-day, as the day's race event began to wind down, boats started anchoring near us in our usually remote part of the bay. Within a couple of hours we found ourselves tucked in the midst of countless boats and our plans for an early departure rapidly evaporating, since we do not have an electric windlass.

The following day, by the time enough boats had departed to allow us the confidence to retrieve our anchor manually, it was nearly time for the race to begin. We brought our anchor aboard and headed west around the point toward Marigot Bay and were no more than a mile or two from our anchorage when the race pack approached us from behind. Here we were, hurriedly motorsailing along with our inflatable dinghy in tow, our wind generator and solar panels and umpteen gerry jugs lashed on deck, as we zig-zagged and maneuvered and as quickly as possible dropped ourselves back through the pack, yet still becoming one of those non-racing and thus unpredictable 'obstacle' boats that racers so much love having in the middle of their race course. We eventually arrived in Marigot Bay where we dropped the hook and hopefully blended into the other anchored cruising boats well before the race ended.

When we were ready to leave St. Martin to head for Antigua, we decided to do it in stages. Since our objective was to stop and visit the remote island of Barbuda on our way to Antigua, we did not have any interest this trip in spending time visiting St. Barts, which was our next island stop to the south. Therefore we decided to stop for a night or two at *Anse de Colombier*, a small bay at the north end of St. Barts. We could sit there under our Q-flag and avoid checking in while we waited for good weather for our crossing. We hopped from anchorage to anchorage along the coast of St. Martin, jumping from Marigot Bay to Simpson Bay and finally to Philipsburg before heading off to St. Barts.

Ile Tintamarre, off French St. Martin

Barbuda has my (Annie) vote for the perfect Caribbean island. Miles and miles of perfect pink-white sand and crystal clear cerulean water. In places we found it challenging threading our way through some reefs and coral heads but less than we might have expected, and it was well worth it.

The day after our arrival, we got together with Chuck and Terri from *Maker's Match* who had crossed with us the previous day. Our crossing from *Anse Colombier* on the north end of St. Barts had been one of our poorer weather decisions of our entire trip. Had we just waited until the next day, instead of the miserable headwind pounding on the fifty mile easterly motorsail, we could have enjoyed a calm, nearly serene, spectacularly beautiful day for our crossing.

We were anchored off Eleven Mile Beach at the north end of Low Bay on the west side of the island. There we found the lowest spot we could find and we carried and slid our reasonably lightweight dinghy with its 15 HP Yamaha engine up the sandy dune, across the top, and into the water of the lagoon which separates the west side of the island from downtown Codrington, the capital, where we needed to check in. This was something of a challenge as we took our big fenders from the boat and kind of rolled the dinghy over them and up and over the top of the beach.

You do need to use care when you land your dinghy ashore

Immigration office in Codrington, Barbuda

here. The beach is quite steep to and if there is any kind of surf running you can damage your dinghy and/or engine or injure yourself. Another couple that was anchored near us had motored their dinghy up the outside of the island to the mouth of the lagoon at the north end and then down the length of the lagoon to town which had taken them several hours.

The trip to Codrington took us about an hour from the time we left our boat. We motored the mile or so across the lagoon to town and walked around the small village. We checked in with the local authorities and had a very good lunch at a small restaurant which had been recommended by the official when we checked in. The restaurant had only four tables, but the meal of lamb and rice was quite good.

If you are looking for tranquility and isolation and perfection, for me (Annie) Barbuda was it. We took our dinghy all around the west and south sides of the island snorkeling and we loved it. We also

Local restaurant – Codrington, Barbuda

spent some of our days walking much of the length of Eleven Mile Beach. There are local tour guides who will take visitors to visit the frigate bird colony which is located in the mangroves of the lagoon. We did not take this tour but heard from some friends that it was fun and, as an added bonus, they were even given some lobster by their tour guide.

Don't expect to do any provisioning here. The town is tiny and there is not even any place to leave your garbage. Keep it aboard and you can offload it when you get to Antigua.

Coco Beach at the southern end of the island offers a pleasant anchorage amidst some huge but scattered coral heads. It is possible to anchor on the sandy bottom and allow your boat to fall back on its chain and come to rest near one of the large coral heads. These widespread coral heads are twenty or thirty feet in diameter and make for interesting snorkeling. Ashore there are a couple of resorts here. The small Coco Point resort was open and seemed to be flourishing while we were there, but the nearby K-Club resort, which had been known as one of the late Princess Diana's retreats, was closed at the time.

Just around the corner from Coco Beach, between Coco Point and Spanish Point to the east, is Grovenor Bay at the very south end of the island. Grovenor Bay is full of large patches and stretches of barrier type reef. Under appropriate conditions you can take your boat and work your way into the bay to drop anchor.

Coco Beach, Barbuda — Spectacular!!

Jolly Harbour – We enjoyed a wonderful sail from Barbuda down to Antigua. We did some fishing with a line over the side on the trip but hooked only one barracuda which we released. Our friends had better success aboard their boat during this crossing and caught a number of tuna. They gave us some for dinner and it was very tasty!

There is a very nice marina with a working yard located in Jolly Harbour, on the western shore of Antigua. We eventually chose to haul our boat here and left it for a year on the hard. The storage yard is located several feet above water level, is tucked back in snugly behind the sheltered harbor, and they strap the boats to the pavement and weld the stands together for added hurricane protection. Upon returning to Antigua the following year to launch the boat we were allowed to paint the bottom ourselves.

Jolly Harbour features a large open air bar/restaurant with good food at fair prices and a large swimming pool with locker rooms and showers available for patrons to use. Wifi is available for a reasonable price. There is a fairly well-stocked grocery store, *The Epicurean*, located in the complex along with a number of smaller shops peddling everything from jewelry, clothing, and local crafts, to beer, wine, and liquor. The grocery store had a good selection of items, but the pricing was such that any kind of major provisioning here would have been substantially more costly than any we had previously encountered.

After a few days in the anchorage outside of Jolly Harbour, we left to meet our friends on the south side of the island. We left early enough to allow us to take the scenic route and circumnavigate the island. We headed up the western shore, across the north side of Antigua past the mouth of St. John's Harbour, where we spent a night anchored in nearby Dickenson Bay off the *Sandals* resort. From there we headed out to Great Bird Island just off the northeast corner of Antigua where we dropped the hook and spent a couple of days enjoying the sun and surf and snorkeling the reefs and exploring this small out-island. The area is a national park that offers pristine water, coral reefs, and a beautiful sandy bottom and beach.

From Great Bird we worked our way out through the nearby reef to the outside and down the eastern shoreline to Nonsuch Bay where we spent a night at anchor before moving on to Falmouth Harbour on the south shore of Antigua. Eric Clapton has a home which is visible as you sail along the eastern shoreline of the island. The eastern shore of Antigua offers a cruising ground that is definitely worthy of more time than we gave it. If we had had our druthers we would have spent another two weeks or more exploring this area.

At anchor off Great Bird Island

While we were in Antigua, as we did when we were anywhere, we used the public transit system. Taxis are available but they are expensive. The bus system is easy to use, relatively quick getting from point A to point B, and cheap. And the locals, both the drivers and the passengers and people on the street, are helpful if you need assistance. We caught the bus from English Harbour and also from Jolly Harbour and rode it into downtown St. John's to go check out a grocery store and also to visit the large indoor farmer's market near the waterfront in St. John's. We picked up the bus just down the street from Nelson's Dockyard when we were at Falmouth and English Harbours, which are right together, and in Jolly Harbour we caught the bus just up the street from *The Epicurean* grocery store, near the casino.

In Antigua, the provisioning choices are much less impressive than further up island. The grocery store at Jolly Harbour (*The Epicurean*) is the same store that you ride the bus into St. John's to visit. The one in St. John's may be a tad larger but we didn't find any significant difference between the two.

As we began to relate earlier, we had come to Antigua specifically to meet up with our good friends MaryLiz (ML) and Chris who were aboard their 32 foot Westsail, *Wandering Albatross*. They had entered their boat in the Antigua Classic Yacht Regatta and, after jumping through all of the requisite hoops, had spiffed up the boat nicely with fresh varnish and a lot of other improvements.

It seems that, thanks to Chris's in-depth knowledge of the Westsail 32, he was able to adequately document the boat's heritage as stemming from a classic wooden boat. The classic wooden boat had been molded into fiberglass by the Westsail people without making any substantial changes to its original design and therefore it qualified as a classic yacht. Anyway, to the best of our understanding, it was something like that.

Several months prior to the race they had invited us to join them as crew for this event. With our limited racing experience (none for Annie; just a couple of seasons racing once weekly and learning the ropes aboard a friend's yacht in Baltimore harbor for David) we were reluctant, but Chris and ML were adamant, so we agreed to participate. The race, which in recent years has been sponsored by *Panerai*, a high end Italian watchmaker, is one of the world's premier classic yacht races and draws boats and crews from around the world.

We first met Chris and MaryLiz in Luperón harbor in the Dominican Republic where we became good friends while spending hurricane season there. We made more than one bus trip together to Santo Domingo and Boca Chica on the south coast of the DR late in the season to escape the confines of our entrapment in Luperón. At the end of hurricane season we departed Luperón only days apart and met up several times thereafter on the south coast of Puerto Rico where we shared both Thanksgiving and Christmas dinners together aboard *Fidelis*.

Falmouth Harbour – We met up with Chris and ML in Falmouth Harbour, which was the home base for the racing fleet for the first half of race week. This harbor is on the south side of the island just a hop, skip, and a jump away from neighboring English Harbour. Falmouth Harbour is a large, well protected circular bay with a huge anchorage and is home to the Antigua Yacht Club along with a number of other marinas and a storage yard.

English Harbour – Home of the world famous Nelson's Dockyard, tiny English Harbour is steeped in so much history and tradition that it's almost palpable. Beautiful gardens, a variety of restaurants, pubs, museums, and small shops, and the Admiral's Inn, converted from an old storage building, offer a pleasant ambiance that we did not find anywhere else on our travels. Across the street from the Admiral's Inn, another old building houses a sail loft, *A & F Sails*, where we had our sails refurbished. For a fair price they did a fine job with some restitching and general maintenance of the sails.

English Harbour, Antigua

For the Antigua regatta, we came down from our hurricane haunts in Puerto Rico and the Virgin Islands. Chris and ML however, who are much more sailing purists (They do have a Solomon Technologies electric motor in their boat which allows them to maneuver in and out of harbors but then must be recharged.), had just arrived in Antigua after a sojourn up through the windward islands where they had spent hurricane season on the hard in Trinidad.

While we were in St. Martin we had met up with our mutual good friends Chuck and Terri aboard *Maker's Match* who had also been invited to crew. They too were members of the Luperón class of 2005 and we had met up with them during Christmas season in the USVI. Then we met up again in St. Martin and had sailed down island together from St. Martin via Barbuda. Chuck and I (David) ended up actually practicing and crewing with Chris and ML aboard the boat, while Annie and Terri served as shore crew, helping to get the boat into and out of its berth at the yacht club.

The weather, as it turned out, played into our hands. Chris and MaryLiz brought along a brand new lightweight Genoa sail that they had had made for the race but had not yet had the opportunity to fly. Surprisingly, we actually ended up using it for every race during the four days of competition. We were placed in the 'Classics A' division, along with eight other classic designs.

The first day of the race we were not going to use the new sail, as Chris felt that the breeze was just a little too heavy for it. However, around the middle of the race the breeze began to fall off enough that he decided a sail change was in order. Our crew was not well-rehearsed as, on our practice sail the previous day the winds had been so light that we had just given up trying to do anything and called it off. Nonetheless, on this first day of the race we went ahead and made the change underway with no significant loss of speed, the only problem being a single wrap in the halyard at the top of the headstay. We tried to catch up with the lead boat, but only managed to close the gap slightly. We crossed the finish line in second place. Later in the evening, however, when results were posted it turned out that we had corrected on handicap to first place.

The second day of racing started out similar to the first with us flying the working jib, however, as we were approaching the start line, Chris decided to go once again with the larger jib and, with just about a minute to the start we furled the working jib, snapped on the new Genoa, and, with less than ten seconds to the gun, had it in place and drawing. The previous day's sailchange had served us well. On this second day of the race we crossed the finish line first in class and had the opportunity to hear the sweet sound of victory with the blast from the winner's gun as we crossed the line.

The third day dawned with a decent breeze that, shortly after the start of the race, just about died away completely. So much so that several of the larger boats that were scheduled to start later actually bowed out of the race. The breeze blew long enough though, to allow us a substantial lead over the rest of our class and we never looked back. Another winning gun and another first place for *Wandering Albatross*.

On the fourth and final day of the regatta, conditions were just different enough to lend the advantage to another boat in our class, *Apsara*, a sweet-looking little ketch. We crossed the finish line second but not close enough to steal the win, even on corrected time.

We had all gone into this race just hoping to make a respectable showing. I know my only hope was that I didn't botch things up too badly and absolutely humiliate myself and the crew. We were just hoping to have fun and make a decent race of it. As it turned out, with weather and conditions that happened to be just about ideal for our boat and with just the right set of sails for those conditions, we not only turned in a respectable performance, we ended up winning our class of 9 boats ('Classic Class A' division) outright and placing third overall among all boats under 40 feet for the week.

We all had a great time during race week and we enjoyed all of the parties and festivities associated with the race. *Panerai* provided hats and shirts to all of the participants in the race and professional photographers were continuously buzzing in and out of the yachts during the race, while helicopters flew above us taking photographs and video. The photos were made available to the participating yachts for purchase after the race was over.

The final night, when we attended the awards ceremony and

the name of the boat was announced, as we walked through the crowd up to the stage to receive our trophies, I heard an anonymous comment from somebody in the crowd that summed up the week for us when he said, "*Wandering Albatross* – that's that little Westsail that kicked everybody's ass!"

Although sailboat racing has never been on our list of pursuits, we were amazed at how much fun and how exciting the week was. For us it unexpectedly turned out that the Antigua regatta happened to be one of the best, most cherished memories of our cruising experience.

FYI, if you happen to be there during the classic yacht race, don't hesitate to look for a spot as crew on the boats. These are some of the most beautiful boats in the world, most of which you would never be able to go aboard even if you paid. But many of the larger boats generally welcome additional hands for these races, even if your sole purpose is as ballast. We encountered a number of cruisers who had joined in as crew on some of the biggest, most beautiful yachts in the race, and they had the time of their lives.

Photo courtesy of Chris & MaryLiz – *Wandering Albatross*

Racing aboard *Wandering Albatross* in the Antigua Classic Regatta

The winning crew, (L-R) Chuck and Terri of *Maker's Match*, MaryLiz and Chris, owners of *Wandering Albatross*, and us in front (note open-mouthed amazement)

The awards ceremony at Nelson's Dockyard

When race week was over, we separated and went our separate ways. Chris and ML headed up toward Barbuda, Chuck and Terri headed toward Guadeloupe aboard *Maker's Match*, and we headed back to Jolly Harbour to have the boat hauled before flying back to the States. It was May.

And so ended our cruising career. After eight years of living aboard and four years in the Caribbean, we flew home for hurricane season to work for a little, visit the family, and to take care of business, intending to return and pick up again where we had left off. But, not terribly unexpectedly, somewhere in the midst of all this, something changed. The end of hurricane season rolled around and we weren't ready to go back. We weren't sure at first, so we kept the boat on the hard for a while and went about with our lives. However, after a year with no change of heart, we decided that our cruising life was over. We knew it would end some day; we were just surprised at how the end snuck up on us.

A year later in April I (David) headed back to Antigua and prepped and launched the boat. I had my cousin Jim (who just a year before we left our boat had sold his catamaran *Chez Freddy*, after he and wife Freddy spent a year cruising the Caribbean) fly in from Denver to crew with me for the trip home. Together he and I spent four weeks sailing back to Florida. It took us four weeks to cover the ground that Annie and I had taken four years exploring. We sailed *Fidelis* back to St. Augustine, Florida where we put her up for sale.

Sun-up, Barbuda

David and Annie LaVigne lived aboard their 37 foot CSY cutter *Fidelis* for eight years. David (Captain Doctor Dave) is a veterinarian who practiced in Michigan with Annie as office manager and technician. In 1999, after 20 years of practice ownership, they sold everything and moved aboard the boat to head to the Caribbean.

Annie and David are relative latecomers to sailing. In 1993 they took a beginning sailing class at Delta College in Bay City, Michigan and before the class was over they bought their first sailboat, a 24-foot trailerable. They bought *Fidelis* in 1997 and in 1999 they moved aboard and left to live their dream. They crossed from the Great Lakes via the Erie Canal and Hudson River and down the east coast. Stopping in the Inner Harbor of Baltimore with the intention of staying for six months, they enjoyed it so much that they stayed for four years while Doctor Dave worked at a veterinary practice and Annie managed HarborView Marina, a large luxury marina on the edge of the Inner Harbor. After two record-setting winters they left the Chesapeake and headed to the Caribbean where they continued to live aboard and cruise for an additional four years.

They are commodores in the Seven Seas Cruising Association (SSCA) and David holds a USCG master's license. As a veterinarian he is author of two books: *Where There Is No Pet Doctor* (previously released as *Wilderness Veterinary Companion for Cruisers and Other Outbackers*) and *Pets On Board? Adapting Your Pet to Travel By Boat or RV*.

Island Hopping to the Caribbean is Annie's and David's second collaborative effort. The shorter version of this book, *Cruising the Islands - Cheapie-Cheapie* was their first. You can contact them at captdrdave@captdrdave.com.

5364034R0

Made in the USA
Lexington, KY
01 May 2010